Creative Metal Crafts

Creative Metal Crafts

25 BEAUTIFUL PROJECTS YOU CAN USE EVERY DAY

Joanna Gollberg

LARK BOOKS
A Division of Sterling Publishing Co., Inc.
New York

EDITOR
Marthe Le Van

ART DIRECTOR
Susan McBride

COVER DESIGN
Barbara Zaretsky

ASSOCIATE ART DIRECTOR
Shannon Yokeley

ASSISTANT EDITORS
Nathalie Mornu,
Anne Hollyfield,
Rebecca Lim

EDITORIAL ASSISTANCE
Delores Gosnell

PHOTOGRAPHY
Keith Wright
keithwright.com

ILLUSTRATION
Orrin Lundgren

PROOFREADER
Sherry Hames

Library of Congress Cataloging-in-Publication Data

Gollberg, Joanna.
  Creative metal crafts : 25 beautiful projects for your home / by
Joanna Gollberg.-- 1st ed.
      p. cm.
Includes index.
  ISBN 1-57990-451-3
  1. Metal-work. I. Title.
  TT205.G67 2004
  745.56--dc22

                                          2003015804

10 9 8 7 6 5 4 3 2 1

First Edition

Published by Lark Books, a division of
Sterling Publishing Co., Inc.
387 Park Avenue South, New York, N.Y. 10016

© 2004, Joanna Gollberg

Distributed in Canada by Sterling Publishing,
c/o Canadian Manda Group, One Atlantic Ave., Suite 105
Toronto, Ontario, Canada M6K 3E7

Distributed in the U.K. by: Guild of Master Craftsman Publications Ltd.,
Castle Place, 166 High Street, Lewes, East Sussex, England BN7 1XU
Tel: (+ 44) 1273 477374, Fax: (+ 44) 1273 478606,
E-mail: pubs@thegmcgroup.com; Web: www.gmcpublications.com

Distributed in Australia by Capricorn Link (Australia) Pty Ltd.,
P.O. Box 704, Windsor, NSW 2756 Australia

The written instructions, photographs, designs, patterns, and projects in this volume are intended for the personal use of the reader and may be reproduced for that purpose only. Any other use, especially commercial use, is forbidden under law without written permission of the copyright holder.

Every effort has been made to ensure that all the information in this book is accurate. However, due to differing conditions, tools, and individual skills, the publisher cannot be responsible for any injuries, losses, and other damages that may result from the use of the information in this book.

If you have questions or comments about this book, please contact:
Lark Books
67 Broadway
Asheville, NC 28801
(828) 253-0467

Printed in Hong Kong

ISBN 1-57990-451-3

Contents

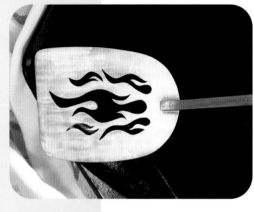

Introduction

It all started with a picture frame. Which led to a spatula. Then to soap dishes and pen holders and pretty soon, I was *hooked* on making metal home accessories. As a professional jeweler, I spend lots of time working with little, tiny pieces of metal. When I decided to branch out, I simply started experimenting with the same material on a slightly larger scale. How wonderful to find that the same easy cold-connecting techniques I use in my jewelry cross over perfectly into making one-of-a-kind home accents, from salad servers to switch-plate covers. Not only is the process a fun challenge, but I also end up with handmade items I can enjoy—and that I actually use every day.

I've picked 25 of my favorite designs and turned them into projects for this book. With step-by-step instructions and how-to photos, I'll show you exactly how to make them for yourself. To complement a variety of decor styles, the projects feature diverse types of metal, such as sterling silver, stainless steel, brass, copper, and aluminum. In several projects I've enhanced the metal with unusual accent materials, such as acrylic, wood, plastic laminate, and pearls. All of the projects are truly functional, and there is something for every room in your home. A copper chopstick rest in the delicate shape of a ginkgo leaf will help you set a tranquil table (see page 38), while a modernist Mail-Call Sorter (see page 78) will help keep you and your home up-to-date. One outstanding feature of the projects is that you can personalize the materials you use to reflect what you like and how you decorate your home. Since *you* are making the projects, *you* can decide what colors and textures you like best.

In the first chapter, The Basics, you'll learn cold metalworking skills such as piercing, sawing, riveting, chasing, sanding, and finishing. Although the names of these techniques may be unfamiliar now, they're all quite easy to understand and apply. You'll never even have to fire up a torch or solder—if you can use a hammer and saw, you're already off to a great start! Learning these procedures is an essential part of metalwork, and practicing them will be part of your creative process.

Don't get discouraged if your first project doesn't turn out perfectly; the next one you make will definitely be better. Your metal-working will continually improve and your skills will grow through repeated application. Dedicate yourself to learning these new skills and the results will be rewarding.

As you develop as a metalworker, I encourage you to actively nurture your creative life. At the end of the book I've included a selection of images from other metalworkers to delight and inspire you. Look closely in stores and through catalogs to see what new accessories you can make for your home. When you go to the crafts store or even when you take a walk in the woods, assess the potential in all types of materials; you may see something unexpected you can include in a home accessory, such as a pipe that becomes a towel bar. You may even consider branching out from the book's projects to develop some of your own. Look through books for design ideas. Images and new shapes appear in all sorts of places, such as children's books and interior design magazines. Once you get an idea, start drawing. Even if you think you can't draw, let go and sketch away! It doesn't matter how "good" you are; you're drawing for yourself, to get ideas flowing, to test design possibilities on paper.

In *Creative Metal Crafts* you'll learn techniques and create projects that will help you to express yourself uniquely and add a distinctive flavor to your environment. With a just a few basic skills you can enter a whole new world of functional metal crafts. If you can think of it, you can make it—let this book be your guide.

The Basics

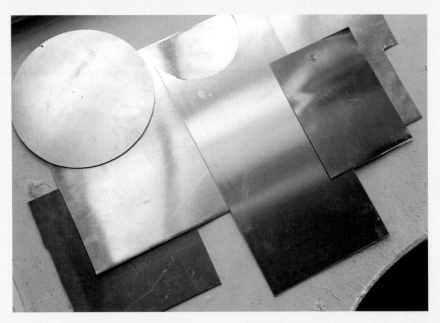

Assorted metals, from left: aluminium (disc), copper, sterling silver, nickel, stainless steel

Not only is metal inherently beautiful, but it's also a versatile material to use to create unique home accessories. We'll explore many different kinds of metals, such as sterling silver, copper, brass, stainless steel, and aluminum. These metals differ in color, strength, and durability, and you can use them in different ways to perform various functions and achieve distinct styles.

Soldering—or using heat—to connect pieces of metal is an advanced skill you won't need to know to accomplish the projects in this book. Instead, you'll be joining metal by much more simple means. Everything is cold connected using easier techniques such as riveting, bending, and sewing. You'll also use basic metalworking skills such as piercing and sawing, drilling, chasing, and finishing.

Many of the techniques used in this book are also used for making metal jewelry. Later, you may wish to make some smaller, wearable pieces with the skills you acquire.

MATERIALS

One of the great advantages of using cold connections is that you have lots of options when choosing the material you want to use in your projects. Cold connecting has very few material limitations, so you can always cleverly adapt the projects. Often metals that are intended for one specific use can be used in these projects in a completely new way. As you will see, aluminum flashing used in roofing can also make a great lampshade (see page 84), and copper tubing used in plumbing can become a beautiful towel bar (page 68).

Aluminium flashing, copper tubing

Metal tubing, metal wire, sheet metal

Metals of different gauges (thicknesses)

Metal

Metal is manufactured in several forms, most notably sheet, wire, tubing, and grain. To make the projects in this book, you'll be using sheet, wire, and tubing. The sheet and wire are measured in a standard gauge system, the American Wire Gauge (AWG) system, also known as the Brown & Sharp (B & S) system. Depending on the manufacturer, metal gauges differ slightly, but not enough to really affect your projects. Gauges inversely indicate the metal's thickness—the higher the gauge number, the thinner the metal. Tubing is measured in millimeters and sized by its outside diameter, commonly abbreviated as *OD*, and interior diameter, or *ID*. A tube's outside diameter is the measurement between its exterior walls. Its interior diameter is the measurement between the interior walls. The measurements in this book are given in both the U.S. and the metric versions, where appropriate, but you must have a metric ruler labeled with millimeters to create these projects. It will be easier for you to count in millimeters, and your work will be more precise.

Sheet metal is always flat, but you can purchase it in many different shapes, such as round discs. You can also buy wire in many shapes such as round, square, half-round, triangular, and bar. Sheet metal and wire are available through metal suppliers, jewelry supply stores, and home improvement centers. Various types of sheet metal are also sold at your local metal scrap yard, often for much less money than at traditional retailers. I highly encourage you to visit your local scrap yard and rummage through their stock. Much of the metal I've used for the projects in this book came from the scrap yard.

Metal wires, tubes, and rods

Color Accents

Many of these metal home accessory projects include vibrant color accents constructed from various kinds of plastics. Acrylic sheet is a great material to use for adding color and dimension to your pieces. You can saw it like metal, though you'll want to do so a bit more slowly to avoid melting the acrylic with the friction heat of the saw blade. You can also file and sand acrylic much like metal. You can buy acrylic sheets at plastics suppliers, home improvement centers, and specialty hardware stores. Kitchen counter laminate samples are also a wonderful source for color accents. You can find these at home improvement centers. Most stores won't mind if you take a few color samples for use in your home accessory projects as long as you first ask permission.

From left: acrylic sheets, laminate samples

TOOLS

The metalworking tools you'll need to create these cold-connected projects are fewer in number and less expensive to purchase than those required for hot metal-work. You can purchase the tools from most jewelry supply outlets, hardware stores, or home improvement centers.

Scribe

A scribe is a pointed metal "pencil" that you use to draw on metal. There are commercially manufactured scribes, but you can also make your own by filing the end of a coat hanger or a nail to a sharp point.

Saw Frame & Saw Blades

A jeweler's saw frame is an extremely handy tool for cutting metal. There are many different saw frames from which to choose. You'll need both a shorter frame with a 3⅛-inch (80 mm) throat and a larger frame with an 8-inch (20.3 cm) throat to accomplish all the projects in this book. There are also many different sizes and kinds of saw blades available. Go ahead and invest in good quality blades; poor quality blades, though less expensive, often break. You'll need size 2/0 or 3/0 saw blades for these projects. (The 3/0 blades are smaller than the 2/0 blades.)

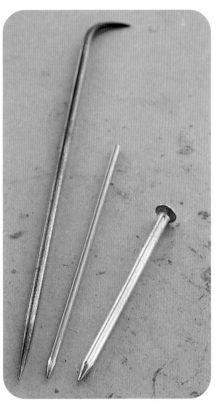

Commercial and homemade scribes

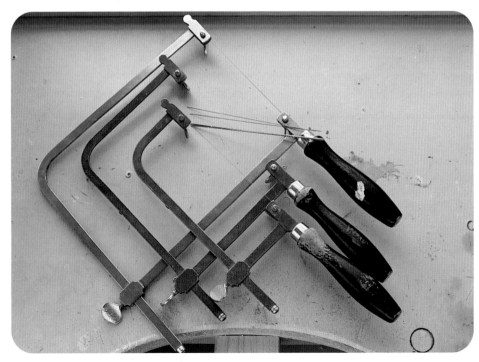

From left: portable bench pin with C-clamp, commercial bench pins

Bench Pin

When sawing metal, you'll place it on top of a bench pin. Bench pins come in many different styles and sizes. If you don't have a jeweler's bench, you'll want a portable bench pin to put on your worktable. Bench pins are sold at jewelry supply stores, or you can make your own with a C-clamp and a flat piece of wood.

Jeweler's saw frames and saw blades

From left: steel blocks, chasing tools and stamps (in cup)

Steel Block

When hammering metal, you'll place it on top of a steel block. Any piece of flat, smooth, polished steel will work as a steel block, or you can buy a classic jeweler's steel block from any jewelry supply house.

Sandpaper (220 & 400 grit)

The type of sandpaper that works best on metal is called *wet/dry sandpaper*, and it's generally gray in color. (The grit on ordinary brown sandpaper isn't affixed well enough to use on metal.) It's helpful to remember that the higher the sandpaper is numbered, the finer its grit.

Flexible-Shaft Machine

The flexible-shaft machine, or *flex shaft* as it's commonly known, is an extremely convenient metalworking tool that functions like a rotary drill. Similar to a sewing machine or an automobile accelerator, the flexible shaft is motorized with different speeds you control with a foot pedal. It has a longer, more flexible shaft and a smaller chuck than a regular drill, which is necessary for inserting accessories such as small drill bits and sanding mandrels.

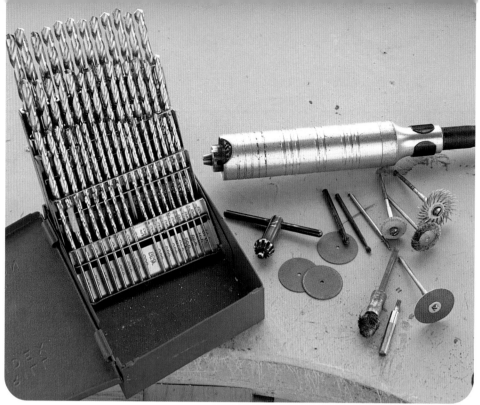

Clockwise from left: assorted drill bits, flexible-shaft machine, flexible-shaft machine accessories, chuck key

Sanding disc (left), plastic bristle disc (right)

Flexible-Shaft Machine Accessories

There are countless flexible-shaft accessories available on the market, such as sanding mandrels, burrs, grinding attachments, and cutting discs. You'll mostly be using your flexible shaft for drilling holes and sanding, but you can certainly have more accessories on hand if you wish.

Drill Bits

You can purchase drill bits individually or as a set in a variety of sizes. It's very useful to have an assortment of drill bits on hand at all times. For the projects in this book, it's important to have metric-sized drill bits. If your drill bits don't exactly match the size of the wire or tubing you're using, it's okay if they're a little bigger. For example, you can use a 1.5-mm bit to drill a hole for 1.45-mm tubing. Make sure that the bits you select are made to be used on metal, not wood.

Chasing Hammer

A chasing hammer is a ball-peen hammer. This means that one side of its head is shaped like a ball, and the opposite side has a flat face like a common hammer. The chasing hammer is smaller than a regular hammer and is specifically weighted for metalwork.

Wooden or Rawhide Mallet

These large flat-faced hammers are well suited for forming metal without distorting the metal surface.

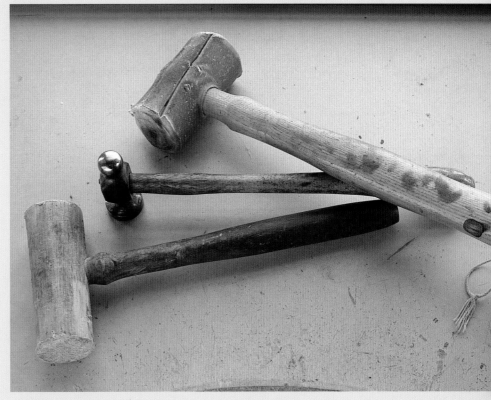

From left: wooden mallet, chasing hammer, rawhide mallet

Center Punch

This can be any kind of tool with a point on one end and a hammering surface on the opposite end. You'll use a center punch for making dimples to use either as decorative marks or prior to drilling holes.

Flaring Tool

This can be any small hand tool that's tapered on one end and flat on the other. I use an old burr, which once was an attachment for my flexible shaft. It's broken off at the end, nicely tapered, and perfect for beginning to open, or *flare*, a piece of tubing for riveting. You can also use a chasing tool that's tapered almost to a point or a large nail. (You must file the tapered end of the nail so there are no snags.)

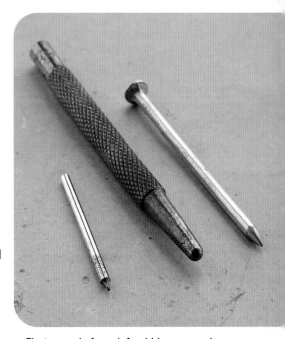

Flaring tools from left: old burr, round-nose chasing tool, nail with filed point

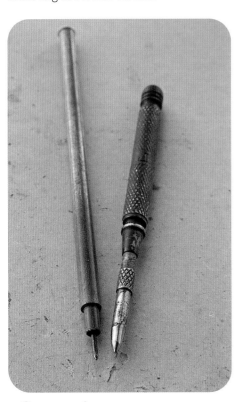

Center punches

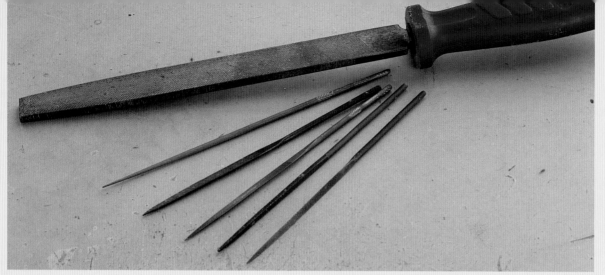

From top: bastard file, assorted needle files

Bastard File

This is a large and inexpensive file you can purchase at any hardware store. It should be fairly coarse, but you should also be able to run your fingers along it without your skin catching on its teeth.

Needle Files

These instruments are for filing small metal parts. They're indispensable because they allow you to file in hard-to-reach places. You'll be using the round, half-round, square, triangular, and barrette needle files. These files look exactly as their names suggest, except for the bar-rette file, which is flat on one side and has no teeth on the other, triangular side. Files remove metal only on the forward stroke. The material is simply scratched on a backstroke, not removed.

Large tapered mandrels

Mandrels

A mandrel is anything you can wrap metal around. Some mandrels are tapered, such as commercial ring and bracelet mandrels, and some remain the same diameter their whole length. You can use anything as a mandrel, even ordinary items you find around your house, such as a dowel or a pencil. Authentic ring and bracelet mandrels, however, are only available through jewelry supply houses.

Assorted tapered mandrels and dowels

Dapping Block & Dap

A dapping block is a wood or steel cube that has different-size depressions on each face. A dap is a domed hand tool used in conjunction with a hammer to push metal into the depressions on the dapping block. A wooden dapping block is much less expensive than a steel dapping block, and I recommend it for use with these projects. There are two kinds of wooden dapping blocks used in this book, a large block with a low depression and a smaller block with multiple faces (see photo, left).

From top: dapping block with multiple depressions, dap, dapping block with low depression

Chasing Tools

Chasing marks are one way to texturize or pattern the surface of metal. You'll use steel chasing tools to make impressions in metal. The tools can be round or square, and they can have an endless variety of shapes carved into their ends. Most jewelry supply houses sell commercial chasing and matting tools. (A *matting tool* is a chasing tool that makes a more complex texture design or imprint on the metal.) You can also make your own tools by filing pieces of scrap steel, such as the end of an old screwdriver. To create a long-lasting, handmade chasing tool, order tool steel, file it into a specific design on one end, and then harden and temper the steel. Handmade tools are fun to make and satisfying to use. A wide variety of commercial

stamps also are available. Sometimes these stamps are made carelessly and their designs are uneven, but you can use needle files to reshape them into their proper design. Keep your eye out at flea markets and junk shops for chasing tools—they often pop up in unexpected places.

Assorted chasing tools, matting tools, and stamps

15

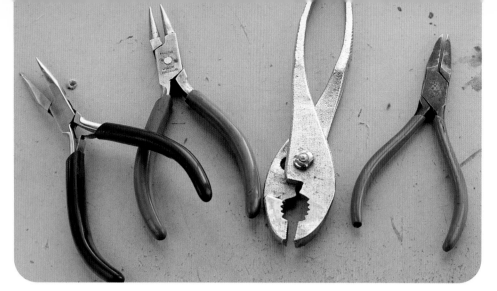

From left: chain-nose pliers, round-nosed pliers, common pliers, flat-nose pliers

Graphite transfer paper (front), tracing paper (rear)

Pliers (Flat Nose, Chain Nose, Round Nose)

These pliers are shaped much as their names imply. The flat-nose pliers have two sides that meet flat on the inside and at a flat angle on the outside of their noses. Chain-nose pliers are flat on the inside, round on the outside, and tapered almost to a point. Round-nose pliers are round inside and out and taper to a point.

Templates

Templates are plastic sheets that have precut and sized holes for tracing. You may want to keep a variety of square-, circle-, and oval-shaped templates on hand. They're great for designing and tracing precise shapes onto metal with a scribe. You can use metric-based templates or templates based on the U.S. measurement system.

Graphite Transfer Paper

This thin sheet of tracing paper is coated with a layer of graphite on one side. It's perfect for transferring a design onto metal. You can purchase graphite transfer paper at art and craft supply stores.

Tracing Paper

Tracing paper is very thin and almost transparent. You can see through it well enough to trace a design from another source. Purchase tracing paper at any art, craft, or office supply store.

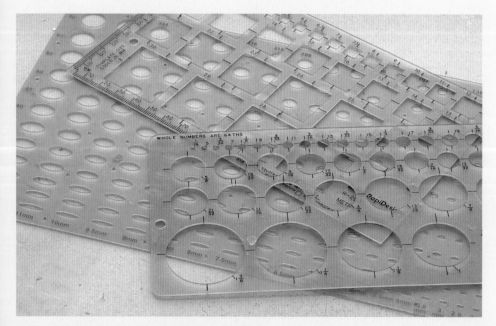

From left: oval, square, and circle templates

Separators

You'll use separators to measure and mark equal distances. You can purchase separators at stores that cater to tool-and-die makers, at machine shops, and from jewelry suppliers.

Digital Calipers

Digital calipers take precise measurements. Unlike analog calipers, this variety provides you with an exact readout. Calipers are great for measuring wire diameter and sheet metal thickness. You can also lock digital calipers at a certain measurement, and then use them as separators.

Stainless Steel Ruler

A stainless steel ruler should have a straight edge that isn't nicked or chipped. It should indicate both inches and millimeters. You may find it useful to have both a short, 6-inch (15.2 cm) ruler and a longer, 12-inch (30.5 cm) ruler.

Permanent Marker

A permanent marker with a fine tip is a great tool for drawing on metal without leaving scratches. Using different colored markers to denote different design areas can also be very helpful.

Safety Glasses

These shatterproof glasses should fit well on your face.

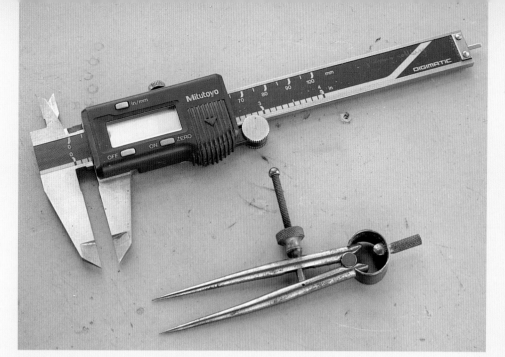

From left: digital calipers, separators

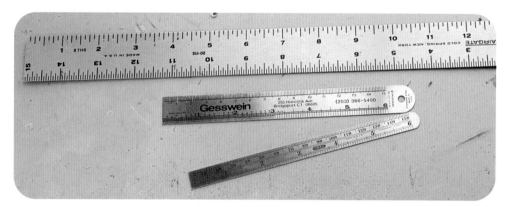

Stainless steel rulers

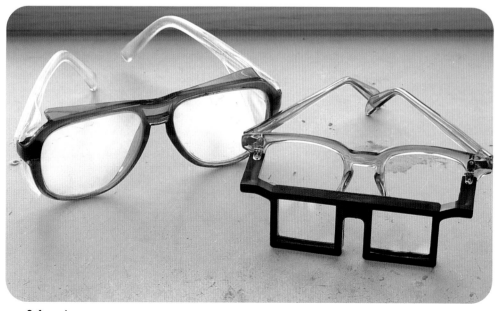

Safety glasses

A NOTE ON TOOLS

If you have access to a professional or a more complete workshop, using three larger, more advanced tools will save you a lot of time. Only invest in these tools if you're sure you'll be using them often. These specialized tools are: a shear with a bending brake, a band saw, and a belt sander. They'll make sawing and filing basic forms a much speedier process.

TECHNIQUES

There are two ways of crafting metal: cold metalwork and hot metalwork. Cold metalworking is easier, faster, and less expensive than learning to solder and setting up a hot metal workshop. It's also equally creative.

Transferring a Design

Once you photocopy a design template from the back of the book, you'll have to transfer the design onto the metal. When transferring any design, conserve as much surface space as possible to conserve metal. Don't start a design in the center of a metal sheet; instead, place the design near its edge or corner. Often, you can use the straight lines of the metal edges to save yourself some sawing.

If the design is geometric in form, you can often use metal rulers, plastic templates, and the scribe to transfer the shapes. If the design is a looser, more organic form, it's best to use graphite transfer paper.

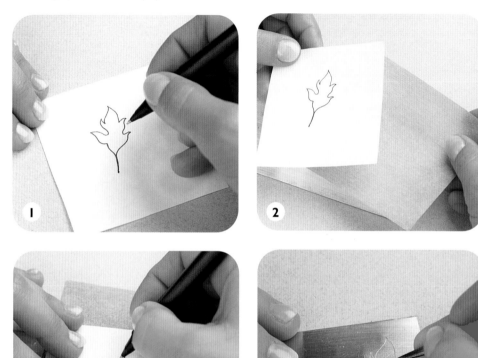

USING GRAPHITE TRANSFER PAPER

1. Photocopy a design template or draw a design on paper.

2. With the graphite-coated side facing down, insert a piece of transfer paper between the design and the sheet metal. You might want to tape the paper down.

3. Trace the design onto the sheet metal with a pencil or the scribe. Remove the graphite transfer paper.

4. Using the scribe, trace back over the design to make sure the transferred lines won't rub off the metal as you work.

USING A CIRCLE DIVIDER TEMPLATE

A circle divider template (figure 1) is extremely useful for marking even spaces around a circle and for determining the x-axis and y-axis of a metal piece. Simply lay the piece on top of the circle divider template, and mark the metal with the scribe. You'll use this template for projects such as the Twig Clock on page 51. You may want to photocopy and laminate your circle template. This way the template is durable and accessible.

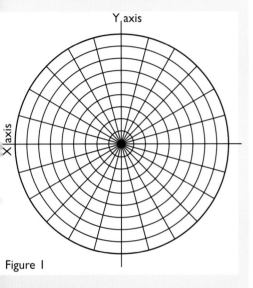

Y axis

X axis

Figure 1

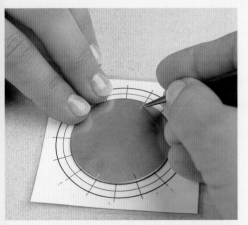

Marking metal with a scribe on a laminated circle divider template

Piercing & Sawing

Piercing and sawing are the first techniques you'll need to know in order to create cold-connected metal home accessories.

INSTALLING A SAW BLADE INTO A SAW HANDLE

1. Open the jaw of the saw frame to a length approximately 10 mm longer than the length of the saw blade.

2. Insert the saw blade into the top nut of the saw frame, with the teeth facing toward you and pointing down. Tighten the nut.

3. Rest the end of the saw frame handle on your sternum, and rest the top edge of the saw frame against the side of your worktable or jeweler's bench.

4. Push the saw handle in with your sternum to slightly shorten the length of the jaw. With the jaw length shortened, place the end of the blade into the lower nut, and tighten. Release the pressure on the handle. The saw blade should be quite taut in the frame.

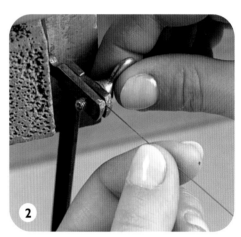

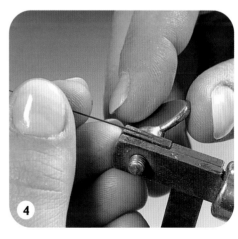

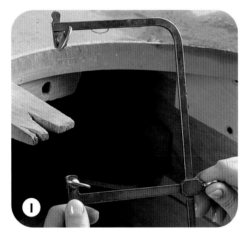

HINT: When installing a saw blade into the frame with the extra long throat, be very careful. This frame has more play in its neck, which can cause the blades to get too tight in the jaw and break.

PREPARING TO SAW

It's helpful to saw near your eye level. This position makes it easier to see what you're doing and saves you from backaches. Either have a short stool for sawing at a table of normal height, or work at a table higher than normal. (Most jeweler's benches are about 1 foot [30.5 cm] taller than regular tables for this purpose.)

SAWING METAL

1. Place the metal on the bench pin.

2. Make one quick run up the metal with the saw blade, using an upwards instead of a downwards stroke. This creates a small indention at the metal's edge and a good place for the saw teeth to bite.

3. Move the saw frame up and down, keeping it at a 90-degree angle to the metal being cut. Keep the frame pointing forward at all times, unless you're turning a sharp corner.

4. For rounding a corner or sawing an arc, turn the metal, not the saw frame.

5. To turn a sharp corner, simultaneously turn the saw and the metal quickly while moving the saw up and down to complete the turn.

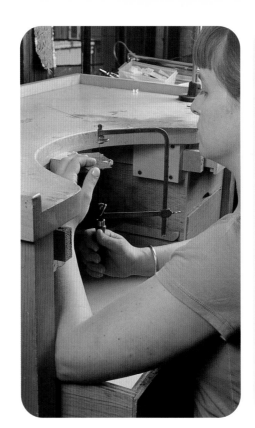

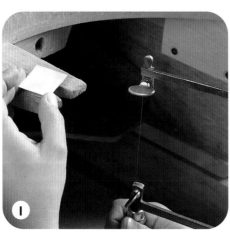

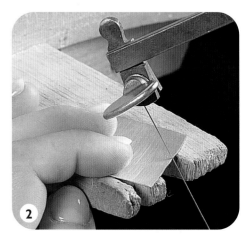

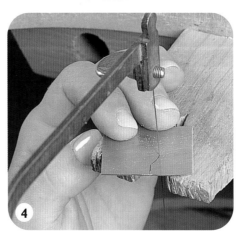

SAWING TIPS

• **Hold the saw lightly in your hand.**

• **For a smooth stroke, run the blade against a block of beeswax prior to sawing.**

• **Let the saw teeth do all the work on the downward stroke.**

• **Use your hand simply as a guide for sawing, not for exerting pressure.**

• **Beginning metalworkers usually break a lot of saw blades. No need to fret if this happens to you—you'll become quite proficient with a little practice.**

• **When using the saw frame with the extra-long neck, the blades can easily break. Be very gentle with any pressure you put on the frame, especially when turning corners.**

PIERCING METAL

To pierce a piece of sheet metal, you'll need a steel block, a center punch, a chasing hammer, a flexible-shaft machine, and an assortment of drill bits. (If you purchase an assortment of bits, you're likely to have just the right size on hand for any hole you need to drill.)

1. Decide where you want to drill a hole. Rest the sheet metal on the steel block. Use the center punch and hammer to lightly indent, or *dimple*, the surface of the metal as shown in photo 1. (The dimple guides the drill bit. If you don't make this indention, the bit can swerve over the sheet metal, making extra marks that would have to be sanded off later. Dimpling before drilling also ensures that the hole is made in the exact location you desire.)

2. Securely insert the drill bit into the flexible shaft. Drill the hole on top of a wooden surface. (You may want to designate one piece of scrap wood as your drilling surface.) Drill with an even, medium speed; do not drill with the motor of the flexible shaft racing or with it creeping along. As shown in photo 2, make sure to keep the drill bit at a 90-degree angle to the metal, or it may break. (If the drill bit breaks and gets stuck in the metal, soak it overnight in a solution of alum and water. This helps dissolve the bit, making it easier to remove.)

3. Thread the saw blade through the drilled hole (see photo 3), attach it to the bottom nut on the saw frame, and tighten the nut. Follow the tips and steps on page 20 to saw interior shapes out of the metal.

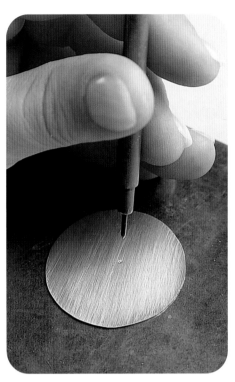

Close up of dimple

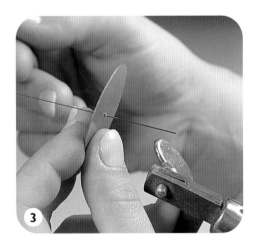

Sanding Metal

There are several techniques for sanding metal. Experiment with each of these methods to find out which one works best for you.

- **Hand-sanding** with sandpaper is the most labor intensive. It also takes much longer to hand-sand metal than it does to use a sanding attachment on the flexible shaft.

- **Sanding discs** snap onto a mandrel attachment for the flexible shaft.

- **Split mandrels** are also made for the flexible shaft. To use one, insert a strip of sandpaper and wrap it around the mandrel.

- **Plastic bristle discs** are relatively new flexible-shaft attachments. These work better for finishing than they do for actually removing metal.

USING A SPLIT MANDREL & SANDPAPER

1. Insert the split mandrel into the flexible shaft. Place a piece of 220-grit sandpaper into the mandrel.

2. Sand the metal surface in one direction to remove scribe lines and deeper marks.

3. Change the sandpaper in the mandrel to a 400-grit. Completely sand back over the metal surface in the opposite direction.

SANDING A TUBING END

You'll often be using very small pieces of tubing to make metal home accessories. To sand their cut ends, it's helpful to hold the tubing with round-nose pliers. Stick one tip of the round-nose pliers into the end of the tubing, and then secure the tubing with the other tip of the pliers as shown below.

SANDING A STRAIGHT EDGE

To sand a straight edge, clip a piece of emery cloth or heavy-grit sandpaper onto a clipboard. The clipboard not only secures the emery cloth but it's also a rigid, flat surface. Using pressure from your hand, rub the edge of a piece of sheet metal back and forth on the emery cloth (see photo, left). Make sure to move the metal slowly so the ends of the straight edge don't become rounded.

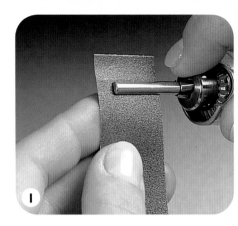

HINT: 220-grit and 400-grit papers are suitable for sanding all of the projects in this book. Some people suggest sanding a metal surface to a 600-grit finish, but this can be an unnecessary step. Experiment sanding to various grits and decide for yourself.

Riveting

A rivet securely traps together two pieces of metal. It passes through layers of metal and then is flared on each side to hold the material. There are two types of rivets: tube and wire. Both types function the same, but look different. Both can be wonderful decorative accents. You can also use rivets strictly to embellish the design of a metal home accessory, as featured in the Shower Curtain Hangers on page 54.

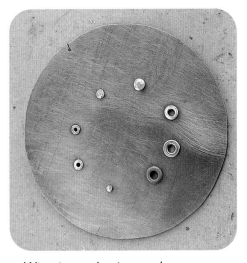

Wire rivets, tube rivets, and a commercial colored rivet

MAKING WIRE RIVETS

WHAT YOU NEED

Digital calipers

Metal sheet

Steel block

Center punch

Chasing hammer

Flexible shaft and accessories

Drill bits

Round metal wire, 14 to 18 gauge

Saw frame and blades

Flat-nose pliers

TIPS FOR MAKING WIRE RIVETS

- **Practice makes perfect. You'll quickly gain control of your rivets by precisely and repeatedly following the step-by-step instructions and tips.**

- **Always use the saw to cut the wire into rivet lengths. Never cut it with the snips. Snips leave an uneven end on the cut wire.**

- **For your first rivet, drill a hole through only one layer of metal and use a large 14- or 16-gauge wire.**

- **Practice riveting several times with thick wire, and then move onto smaller gauges. Never use wire thinner than 20 gauge to make rivets. It simply isn't strong enough.**

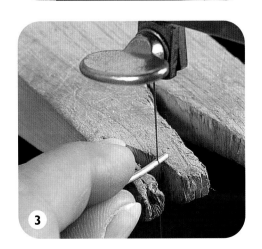

WHAT YOU DO

1. Use the digital calipers to measure the thickness of the metal sheet you want to rivet.

2. Decide where you want to place the rivet. Dimple the metal at this point, and then drill a hole through it (see photo 2). Choose a bit that will make a hole the same diameter as the round wire you plan to use for the rivet.

3. Use the saw to cut a length of wire about 2 mm longer than the thickness of the metal sheet.

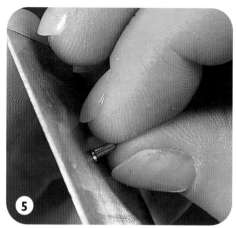

4. Hold the wire in the flat-nose pliers, and sand the cut ends with 400-grit paper.

5. Thread the wire through the hole drilled in step 2.

6. Place the threaded metal on top of the steel block. Use the chasing hammer to gently tap the end of the wire two or three times.

7. Turn over the metal piece. Adjust the length of the rivet wire so there's an equal amount extending beyond each side of the hole (see photo 7). Make two or three gentle taps on the rivet wire, and then turn the piece over again.

8. Repeat turning and tapping the metal (steps 6 and 7) until the wire ends "mushroom," forming the rivet and securing the metal.

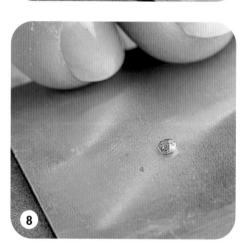

HINT: After mushrooming, use a cup burr attachment on a flexible shaft to make the rivet head round and more uniform in appearance (see photo, left). Cup burrs have teeth on the inside of the cup, and can be purchased from a jewelry supply house.

TROUBLESHOOTING

If the wire bends before the rivet is complete, you may have cut the rivet wire too long. The other possibility is that you didn't turn over the rivet enough times to rivet the wire ends in equal amounts. In wire riveting, it's essential to keep turning the piece over and mushrooming the ends in equal amounts. You absolutely cannot completely mushroom one wire end and then turn the piece over and mushroom the other end.

MAKING TUBE RIVETS

WHAT YOU NEED

Digital calipers

Sheet metal

Steel block

Center punch

Chasing hammer

Flexible shaft and accessories

Drill bits

Metal tubing, 3- to 4-mm OD, and other assorted diameters for practice

Saw frame and blades

Flaring tool

WHAT YOU DO

1. Use the digital calipers to measure the thickness of the metal sheet you want to rivet.

2. Decide where you want to place the rivet. Dimple the metal at this point, and then drill a hole through it (see photo 2). Choose a bit that will make a hole the same diameter as the tubing you plan to use for the rivet.

3. Use the saw to cut a length of tubing about 3 mm longer than the thickness of the metal.

4. Sand the cut ends of the tubing with 400-grit paper (see photo 4). Thread the tube through the hole drilled in step 2.

5. Place the threaded metal piece on top of the steel block. Insert the flaring tool into one end of the tubing. Using the chasing hammer, make one light tap on the flaring tool as shown in photo 5.

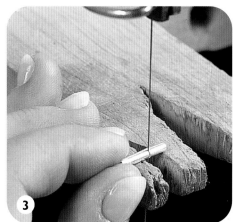

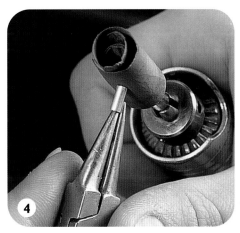

TIPS FOR MAKING TUBE RIVETS

• **Practice, practice, practice. Practice making tube rivets just as much as you practiced making wire rivets.**

• **Start with tubing that has an outside diameter (OD) of 3 to 4 mm, and then rivet larger and smaller tubing to feel how different tubing responds to the flaring tool and to the chasing hammer.**

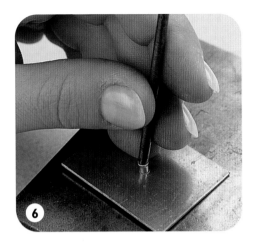

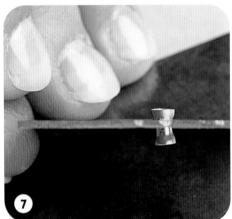

6. Turn the metal piece over. Insert the flaring tool into the end of the tubing, and make one light tap.

7. With the flaring tool and chasing hammer, continue making one tap at a time on each end of the tubing until you can't remove the tubing from the drilled hole (see photo 7). Always equalize the tubing lengths extending from the hole prior to hammering.

8. Continue to flare the tubing without using the flaring tool. Make gentle taps directly on the tubing with the ball side of the chasing hammer (see photo 8). Make sure to continually turn the piece over to tap an equal amount on both sides. Tap the tubing until the rivet is secure.

TROUBLESHOOTING

- **If the tube rivet isn't evenly flared, you may have cut the tubing too long, or you may not have flared the tubing properly.**

- **If the tube rivet splits open, you either hammered too much, hammered too fast, or hammered with too much force.**

- **If the flared tubing is different lengths, you didn't equalize the length of the tubing each time you turned the piece over.**

PRE-FLARING TUBE RIVETS

To make riveting in hard-to-reach places easier, you can pre-flare one side of a tube rivet.

1. Place the cut and sanded piece of tubing on the steel block.

2. Using the flaring tool and chasing hammer, gently tap the end of the tube. (Make sure not to tap too hard, or you'll compress the tubing end resting on the steel block.)

3. Once a nice flare is started on one end of the tubing as shown in photo 3, you can finish it when you flare the other tube end with the chasing hammer.

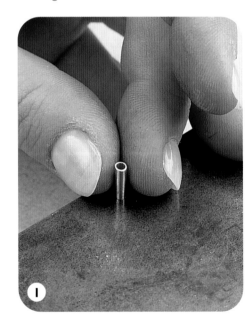

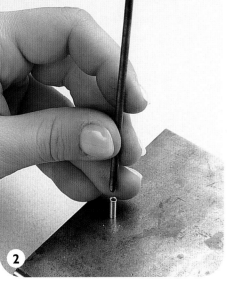

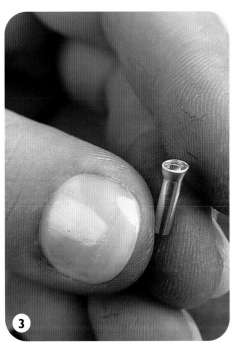

2

MAKING MULTIPLE RIVETS

When making multiple rivets on a circle, it's a good practice to use the "clock" method shown in figure 2. Begin riveting at 12 o'clock (1); then rivet at 6 o'clock (2); then at 9 o'clock (3); then at 3 o'clock (4); and so on. Riveting diagonally across the circumference of a circle helps to secure the metal pieces in the proper position.

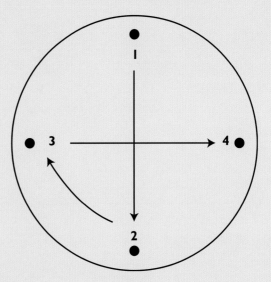

Figure 2

Similarly, when riveting multiple rivets on a square or rectangle (see figure 3), begin with one corner (1), and then rivet the opposite corner (2). Rivet the third corner (3) horizontal to your first rivet, and finish up with the remaining corner (4).

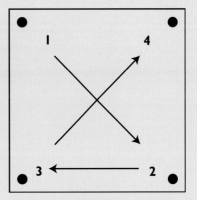

Figure 3

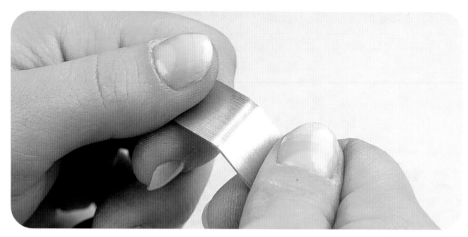
Brittle work-hardened aluminium

Work Hardening

Work hardening is a term used to describe the actual compression of metal molecules when the metal is worked. This "work" can be as simple as bending or hammering. Working any type of metal makes it harder and, in some cases, brittle (see photo, above). You can use this characteristic to your advantage, but keep in mind, especially when you work with thinner metal sheets, that repeated bending can often break the material.

Chasing

Chasing lets you make imprints into sheet metal without removing any metal. To add chasing to a metal surface, you'll need chasing tools, a chasing hammer, and a steel block. You can design a metal home accessory with chasing as the central focus, or you can add a bit of chasing here and there for extra interest or texture. Feel free to add chasing wherever you think it will enhance your project's appearance.

A variety of chased designs

CHASING & STAMPING METAL

1. Rest the sheet metal on the steel block (see photo 1). Because it gives resistance to the hammer blows, the steel block is essential to this process. Otherwise, the metal may become deformed, and the stamp or chasing tool won't properly do its job.

2. Hold the chasing tool in your fingers, and lightly tap it on the metal with the chasing hammer (see photo 2). Experiment by making light and hard hammer taps to see the different impressions you can make.

3. After chasing, the sheet metal may be slightly domed. To flatten the metal, turn it over on the steel block with the chasing facing down. Lightly hammer the surface with a wooden or rawhide mallet as shown in photo 3. (This type of hammer is great for moving and shaping metal without leaving unwanted imprints on the surface.) You may need to repeat this step several times during one chasing session.

HINT: When using commercial stamps, multiple hammer taps are usually required to imprint the metal. Make firm taps with the chasing hammer while rocking the stamp back and forth to imprint the whole design.

Finishing Metal

Finishing is an important part of metal work. The finish of the piece can enhance and complete the design of a home accessory. Metal can be matte, shiny, or have a patina, a coloration or blackening of the metal. There are many finishing options and several ways to achieve each surface effect.

Metal finishes from left: matte, patinaed, shiny

From left: fine-grit steel wool, green kitchen scrub, 400-grit wet/dry sandpaper

Clockwise from left: polishing cloth, steel wool, steel brushes

Clockwise from left: liver of sulphur, selenium toner, black patina solution

Desired Finish	Tools & Materials	Process
MATTE	• 400-grit wet/dry sandpaper • fine-grit steel wool • green kitchen scrub	• rub back and forth or in a circular motion on the metal surface
SHINY	• steel brushes • polishing cloth • coarse steel wool • fine-grit steel wool (for plastic)	• use the steel brushes in the flexible shaft • hand-rub a metal surface with the polishing cloth or the coarse steel wool • hand-rub a plastic surface with the fine-grit steel wool
PATINAED	• selenium toner (from the photography supply store) • liver of sulphur (from jewelry suppliers) • commercial black patina solution (from jewelry suppliers)	• follow the manufacturer's instructions

PATINAS

You can create color finishes on metal, using agents such as liver of sulphur and selenium toner. If you've added a chased design to your piece, a patina makes it more visible.

ADDING A LIVER OF SULPHUR PATINA

You can blacken brass, copper, or silver by dropping the metal into a liver of sulphur solution. This very simple process adds depth and color to your metalwork. Liver of sulphur has a strong odor, so you should use it outside or in a well-ventilated area.

1. In a glass bowl, dissolve one chunk of liver of sulphur in hot water.

2. Drop the metal work into the solution and leave it until the piece turns black, usually 1 to 2 minutes. (If you leave the piece in the liver of sulphur solution too long, the black color becomes a thick crust which will later flake off the metal surface.)

3. Remove the metal from the liver of sulphur solution (see photo 3), and wash it in hot water. The hot water helps the patina adhere to the metal. If needed, repeat this process to create a blacker coating.

4. Leave the metal piece completely black, or rub it with an abrasive such as steel wool, a coarse cleanser, or a green kitchen scrub. This extra rubbing gives the metal a nice final finish, restoring the natural metal color on the highest surfaces as shown in photo 4.

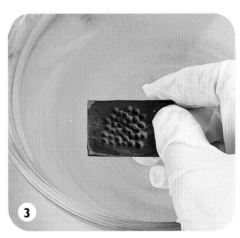

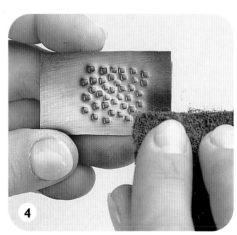

ADDING OTHER BLACK PATINAS

You can use other chemical solutions to make a black patina on metal. Selenium toner is a chemical sold at photography supply stores. Other commercial blackening patinas are manufactured for the jewelry industry and sold by suppliers.

1. Wearing rubber gloves and working in a well-ventilated area, pour the solution into a glass bowl. Drop the metal piece into the solution (see photo 1) and wait about 15 seconds.

2. Using copper tongs or a piece of copper wire, remove the metal from the solution as shown in photo 2. (You should never touch these chemicals with your hands.) Wash the metal in warm water. Repeat this process as needed to create a blacker patina.

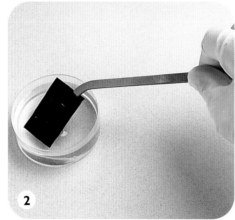

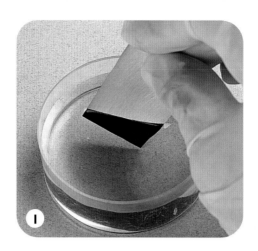

Design

In this book, I give you projects and detailed instructions for replicating them exactly. But chances are, once you get started, you'll want to begin tailoring projects and even creating your own designs. Easy enough! Just get some ideas down on paper.

Designers draw fearlessly. If you lack confidence in this area, there are many simple ways to develop your skills. One method is to look at books, trace the illustrations, and then take small sections of the traced design and make them your own. Change the figures into a design more specific to your needs. You can also look at books of old carpet and fabric design, or even architectural drawings, for your graphic inspiration. Often wildlife reference books have pictures you can alter into fascinating designs for home accessories. The more your projects come from your own creative inspiration, the happier they'll make you.

The Projects

Glowing Votive Holder

An ingenious tab-and-slot system holds a copper cylinder to a base,
forming an ethereal holder for votive candles.

WHAT YOU NEED

Graphite transfer paper

Photocopied templates, page 1

Copper sheet, 24 gauge

Saw frame and blades

Steel block

Center punch

Chasing hammer

Flexible shaft and accessories

Drill bits

Bastard file

Needle files

**Round or tapered mandrel, 2
inches (5 cm) or less in diamete**

Flat-nose pliers

Rawhide or wooden hammer

**Finishing tool or material
of your choice**

Clear spray lacquer (optional)

WHAT YOU DO

1. Use the graphite paper to transfer photocopied template A onto the copper sheet. (Make sure to conserve space on the metal.) Use the saw to cut out the tabbed rectangle, and then pierce and saw out all the decorations and holes. File all the cut edges with the bastard file and needle files.

2. Use the graphite paper to transfer photocopied template B onto the copper sheet. Saw out this piece and file its edges.

3. Sand both copper pieces to a 400-grit finish.

4. Use your fingers to bend the tabbed copper rectangle around the round or tapered mandrel. Make the metal as round as you can, but don't worry about it being perfect.

5. Align the tabs with the slots. Insert the tabs into the slots by slightly bending them over with your fingers. Make sure the straight edges on both rectangle ends meet precisely, and then use your fingers and/or flat-nose pliers to bend the tabs over to complete the connection as shown in photo 1. (You can cover the jaws of the pliers with masking tape to avoid making unnecessary marks on the metal.)

6. Place the copper tube on the round mandrel. Gently hammer it into shape with the rawhide or wooden mallet. Firmly hammer on top of the bent tabs to secure them and to make them flat against the curved metal.

7. Place the copper tube on top of the tabbed circle cut out in step 2. Use the flat-nose pliers to bend up the circle's tabs into a U shape. Insert the bent tabs into the holes at the base of the copper tube. Use pressure from the pliers to make sure the tabs are firmly in place inside the tube of the votive holder. Rest one side of the pliers' jaws on the curved U of the tabs and the other side of the pliers on the bottom of the circle as shown in photo 2. Squeeze the jaws together to secure the connection.

8. Give the votive holder a final finish. The circular marks on the surface of this piece were made with a bristle brush attachment on the flexible shaft. Leave the metal surface open to achieve a natural patina, or spray it with clear lacquer to preserve the bright and untarnished copper color.

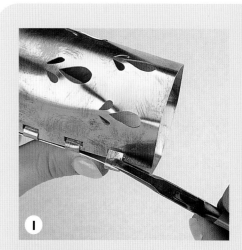

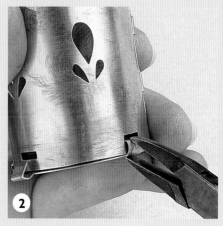

Bubble Switch-Plate Cover

It's simple and fun to create a metal switch-plate cover; choose any color of acrylic to match your style.

WHAT YOU NEED

Photocopied templates, pages 116 and 117

Graphite transfer paper

Scribe

Nickel silver sheet, 24 gauge

Acrylic sheet, ⅛ inch (3 mm) thick, color of your choice

Saw frame and blades

Bastard file

Needle files

Flexible shaft and accessories

Steel block

Center punch

Chasing hammer

Drill bits

Finishing tool or material of your choice

Sterling silver tubing, 2.75-mm OD, 2-mm ID

Steel ruler

Flaring tool

BEFORE YOU BEGIN

A typical switch-plate cover is 2½ x 4¼ inches (6.4 x 10.8 cm). If you want to design your own switch-plate cover, draw a rectangle with those dimensions on a piece of paper, and then freely draw whatever shape you like as long as it meets or exceeds that size. You could also make a classic rectangle, and then rivet on other forms.

WHAT YOU DO

1. Use the photocopied templates and the graphite paper to transfer the bubble designs onto the nickel silver and the acrylic. Saw out these three shapes. File and sand the cut edges.

2. Using the template as a guide, trace the rectangular switch-plate hole onto the top (smallest) nickel silver piece. Pierce and saw out this hole. Mark, dimple, and drill the screw holes for attaching the switch-plate cover to the wall. Finish each layer of the switch plate as desired. (You can achieve this specific finish by rubbing the metal in a circular motion with a fine-grit steel wool.)

3. On the top nickel silver layer (the smallest bubble), use the center punch to dimple four points around the rectangular switch-plate hole, in the positions indicated on the template. Use a 2.75-mm bit to drill the rivet holes at the dimpled points.

4. Use the saw to cut four pieces of the sterling silver tubing, each approximately 1/4 inch (6 mm) long. Sand the cut ends with 220-grit sandpaper.

5. Align the switch-plate layers, placing the acrylic layer between the top and bottom nickel silver layers. Using the top layer's rivet holes as a guide, drill through all three switch-plate layers. Thread one 6-mm piece of tubing through one drilled hole, and rivet. One at a time, continue drilling and riveting the rest of the holes around the rectangular switch-plate hole. (Always rivet opposite the last rivet made as explained in The Basics section, page 27.)

6. At the two points where the switch-plate cover will be attached to the wall, drill through all three layers, using the drill holes in the top layer as a guide.

7. Inside the switch-plate rectangle cut out of the top nickel silver layer, drill a hole through the acrylic layer and rear nickel sheet layer. Saw out these layers and file this new hole flush with the top nickel silver layer.

Ginkgo Leaf Chopstick Rest

The graceful shape of the ginkgo leaf gives this copper chopstick rest its unique profile.

WHAT YOU NEED

Photocopied template, page 117

Graphite transfer paper

Scribe

Copper sheet, 24 gauge

Saw frame and blades

Needle files

Chasing tool of your choice

Chasing hammer

Steel block

Copper tubing, 2.25-mm OD, 1.75-mm ID

Copper tubing, 3.25-mm OD, 2.25-mm ID

Flexible shaft and accessories

Center punch

Drill bits

Commercial patina solution, black (optional)

Flaring tool

NOTE: Directions are for a single chopstick rest. Repeat the steps to make more.

WHAT YOU DO

1. Use the photocopied template with the graphite transfer paper and scribe to transfer two ginkgo leaf designs onto the 24-gauge copper sheet. Conserve space on the metal when transferring the design. Saw out the shapes, and then file the cut edges with the needle files.

2. Use a chasing tool to create texture on the edges of the leaves (see photo 1). Chase the texture on both sides of the metal. (An old flathead screwdriver marred at the ends was used to create the chased texture on this chopstick rest.)

3. Use the saw to cut a 1-inch-long (2.5 cm) piece of the smaller copper tubing. Cut a piece of the larger copper tubing that's approximately ⅞ inch (2.2 cm) long. Sand the cut ends flat.

4. On each copper ginkgo leaf at the mark shown on the template, dimple and drill a hole with a 2.25-mm bit.

5. If you want to give the ginkgo leaves a black patina, do so now. (These leaves were blackened with a commercial patina solution that was rubbed off the surface with a green scrubby. The solution left the chased areas, or depressions in the copper, dark.)

6. Thread the larger tubing onto the smaller tubing. Place each end of the smaller tubing into a ginkgo leaf as shown in photo 2. Rivet the protruding ends of the small tubing with care. When riveting with such a long tube separator, you must hammer gently, and be sure to hammer one side and then the other. This ensures that you won't bend the copper tubing when hammering. (Refer to page 25 for tube riveting instructions.)

7. Turn the ginkgo leaves in the same direction to make sure the chopstick rest sits flat on the table. Firmly tap the rivet ends to secure the leaves in place.

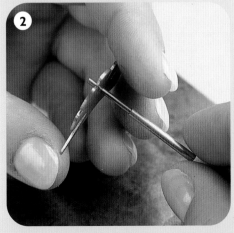

Alluring Aluminum Bath Set

*Chase, rivet, and bend strips of aluminum to construct an
artful setting for soaps and toothbrushes.*

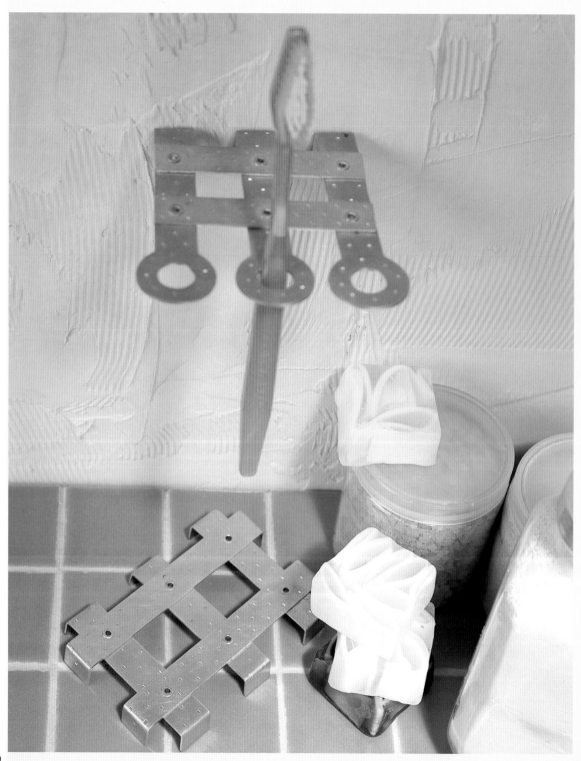

SOAP DISH

WHAT YOU NEED

Saw frame and blades

Aluminum sheet, 18 gauge

Metal ruler

Bastard file

Steel block

Chasing tool of your choice

Chasing hammer

Dividers

Scribe

Center punch

Flexible shaft and accessories

Drill bits

Rawhide or wooden mallet

Steel wool

Aluminum tubing, 3.25-mm OD, 2.25-mm ID

Flaring tool

WHAT YOU DO

1. Use the saw to cut the aluminum sheet into two strips, each ⅝ x 5 inches (1.6 x 12.7 cm). Cut three additional aluminum strips, each ⅝ x 3 inches (1.6 x 7.6 cm). Use the bastard file to round the corners of each metal strip.

2. Use a chasing tool to create a surface decoration on each strip. (You can use whatever design appeals to you. These strips were chased with a tool that has a small square dot on its end.) Place the metal on top of the steel block and chase the strip design using firm and even blows with the chasing hammer.

3. Open the dividers to ¼ inch (6 mm), and mark a centerline down the length of all five strips on their unchased side.

4. From one end of the 5-inch (12.7 cm) strips, measure down 1¼ inches (3.2 cm), 2¾ inches (7 cm), and 4¼ inches (10.8 cm), and mark these locations with the scribe on the centerline. Dimple each mark on both strips, and then drill each dimple with a 3.25-mm bit.

5. From both ends of each of the three 3-inch-long (7.6 cm) strips, measure in 1¼ inches (3.2 cm), and mark these locations with the scribe on the centerline. Dimple, and then drill holes at each point with a 3.25-mm bit.

6. On the unchased side of each aluminum strip, use the scribe to draw a line ½ inch (1.3 cm) in from each end. These are your guidelines for bending the strips.

WHAT YOU NEED

Saw frame and blades
Aluminum sheet, 18 gauge
Metal ruler
Needle files
Bastard file
Flexible shaft and accessories
Scribe
Circle divider template
Circle template
Steel block
Center punch
Chasing hammer
Drill bits
Chasing tool of your choice
Aluminum tubing, 2.7-mm OD, 2-mm ID
Flaring tool
Rawhide or wooden mallet

7. Place one strip on the steel block with its scribed lines facing down. (With the strip in this position, the guideline won't have to be cleaned off later.) Align the scribed line with the steel block's edge. Gently hammer the metal with the rawhide or wooden mallet to make a clean 90-degree angle. Begin hammering right on the strip's curve as shown in photo 1, and then hammer on each plane of the metal until the correct angle is achieved. Repeat this process to bend each end of each aluminum strip.

8. Finish the surface of the metal by rubbing each aluminum strip with steel wool.

9. Use the saw to cut six pieces of 3.25-mm aluminum tubing, each approximately 4 to 5 mm long. File or sand the cut ends flat.

10. Arrange the strips with the two longer ones resting on top of the three shorter ones. Thread one piece of the cut tubing through two aligned drill holes, and rivet. Repeat this process, riveting one short strip at a time, until all the pieces are fastened together.

11. At this stage, the legs of the soap dish don't sit flat. The long strips are positioned on top of the short strips, making the legs slightly uneven. To correct this problem, gently push down on the center of the soap dish as shown in photo 2. Slightly bend the metal until all legs sit evenly on the ground. This quick fix not only solves the problem of uneven legs, but also makes the soap dish into a more functional form.

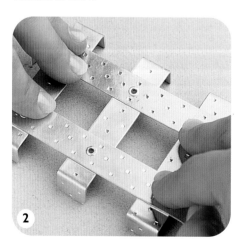

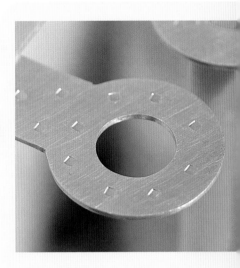

WHAT YOU DO

1. Use the saw to cut two strips of the aluminum sheet, each ½ × 3¼ inches (1.3 × 8.3 cm). File or sand the cut edges straight and smooth. Slightly round the corners of the strips with the bastard file, and then sand.

2. Use the scribe to draw three 1⅛-inch (2.9 cm) circles on the aluminum sheet. Draw them near each other to conserve space. Use the circle divider template to mark the x-axis and the y-axis on each circle. Extend one side of each y-axis line to make it approximately 4½ inches (11.4 cm) long (see figure 1, line A).

3. Measure ¼ inch (6 mm) out from each side of one circle's y-axis, and draw lines out from the circle's edge. Extend these lines out from the circle to make a 3½-inch-long (8.9 cm) rectangle (see figure 1, lines B and C). Repeat this process for each marked circle. Pierce and saw out each aluminum piece.

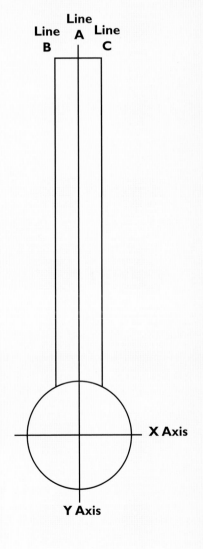

Figure 1

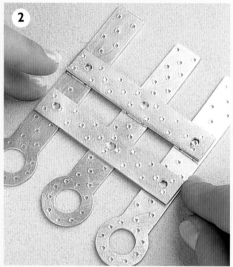

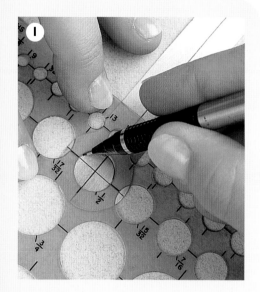

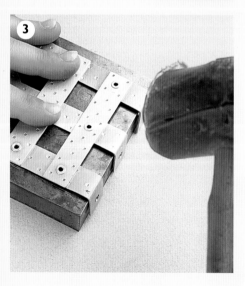

4. File and sand each piece sawed out in step 3 so the rectangles have straight edges and the circles are perfectly round. Slightly round any sharp edges with the bastard file.

5. As shown in photo 1, use the circle template and the x-axis and y-axis marks to center a ½-inch (1.3 cm) circle inside each 1⅛-inch (2.9 cm) circle. Scribe the smaller circles onto the metal, and pierce and saw them out. Sand or file the cut edges to make the interior circles perfectly round.

6. Select the chasing tool of your choice to make decorative marks on the metal. You can create a random design or a more structured pattern on the pieces. (These strips were chased with a tool that has a small square dot on its end.) Chase the design on the metal on top of the steel block, using firm and even blows with the chasing hammer.

7. On each of the 3¼-inch-long (8.3 cm) aluminum rectangles, measure and mark centered points ⁵⁄₁₆ inch (.8 cm), 1⅝ inches (4.1 cm), and 2⅞ inches (7.2 cm) in from one end. Dimple, and then drill all of the marks with a 2.7-mm bit.

8. Arrange the two 3¼-inch (8.3 cm) straight aluminum strips on top of the three strips with the circle ends. Rest one straight strip 1¼ inch (3.2 cm) in from the squared end. Position the second straight strip ½ inch (1.3 cm) in from the first one (see photo 2). Using the drilled holes on the straight strips as a guide, mark corresponding holes on the strips with the circle ends. Dimple and drill these holes with a 2.7-mm bit.

9. Use the saw to cut six pieces of the aluminum tubing, each 4 to 5 mm long. Sand the cut ends flat. Rivet together the top and bottom aluminum strips, making sure to rivet opposite sides in succession and to end with a middle rivet.

10. Use a 3-mm bit to drill a centered hole ⅝ inch (1.6 cm) in from the end of each of the longer aluminum strips. These are the screw holes for fastening the toothbrush holder to the wall.

11. Use the scribe to mark a line on the back side of each of the longer metal strips. Make each line ½ inch (1.3 cm) in from the strip's square end. Place the toothbrush holder on the steel block, and align these marks with its edge. Use your fingers to gently bend over the strip ends. As shown in photo 3, use the rawhide or wooden mallet to finish bending the metal strips into uniform 90-degree angles.

Carved Drawer Pulls

Sparkling metal discs threaded onto a bolt and separated by nuts make fabulous drawer pulls.

WHAT YOU NEED

Circle template

Scribe

Aluminum sheet, 18 gauge

Saw frame and blades

Brass sheet, 24 gauge

Bastard file

Needle files

Circle divider template

Center punch

Steel block

Chasing hammer

Flexible shaft and accessories

Drill bits

Brass bolt, 2 inches (5 cm) long

Finishing tool or material of your choice

8 brass nuts to fit bolt

Flathead screwdriver

Pliers

NOTE: Directions are for a single drawer pull. Repeat the steps to make more.

WHAT YOU DO

1. Use the circle template and scribe to draw two circles on the aluminum sheet. Make one circle 15 mm in diameter and the second 30 mm in diameter. Saw out these circles.

2. Use the circle template to draw a circle on the brass sheet that's 25 mm in diameter. Saw out this circle.

3. File the edges of each metal circle with the bastard file. Be careful not to over-file the circles, or their shapes will distort.

4. As shown in photo 1, use the needle files to create designs on the edges of each circle. To see what each file can do, you may want to experiment first on scrap sheet metal. (The triangular file and the round file create fantastic marks.) Space the marks by eye or by precise measurement; feel free to be as loose or as exacting as you like.

5. Find the center of each circle by placing them on the circle divider template. Draw their x-axis and y-axis with a pencil. Dimple the center mark, and then drill a hole the same size as the brass bolt's diameter.

6. Give each metal circle a final finish. These circles were rubbed with a fresh piece of 220-grit sandpaper.

7. Thread the 15-mm circle on the brass bolt, and then add a brass nut. Use the screwdriver and the pliers to firmly secure the nut on the bolt, trapping the 15-mm circle in place. Add the 25-mm circle and another nut to the bolt, and secure. Add the 30-mm circle and five more nuts. (These five nuts act as spacers, giving your fingers room to grab the drawer pull once it's on the drawer.) Tightly secure all the nuts (see photo 2).

8. Use the last nut to secure the drawer pull to a drawer. Thread the drawer pull through the hole in the drawer, and then tighten this nut on the inside.

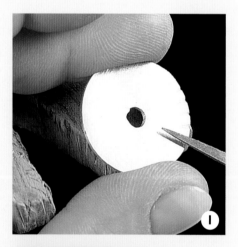

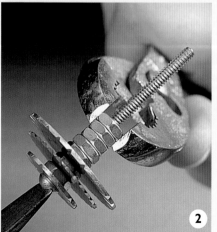

Pushpin Pizzazz

Even a tiny pushpin can get a fresh new look by pairing sensational plastic colors with metal.

WHAT YOU NEED

Photocopied templates, page 119

Nickel silver sheet, 24 gauge

Graphite transfer paper

Scribe

Saw frame and blades

Steel block

Center punch

Chasing hammer

Flexible shaft and accessories

Drill bits

Bastard file

Needle files

Plastic laminate samples, colors of your choice

Finishing tool or material of your choice

Snips

Sterling silver round wire, 18 gauge

Commercial pushpins with flat round heads*

*Purchase pushpins with very thin heads. The inexpensive variety with a removable plastic coating works best. More expensive pushpins have thick heads and won't work in this project.

WHAT YOU DO

1. Decide how many pushpins you want to make. For the front and back layer of each pin, transfer the shapes from the photocopied templates onto the 24-gauge nickel silver sheet. Remember to conserve space on the sheet metal.

2. Pierce and saw out the front layers of the pushpins. Saw out the back pushpin layers on the dotted line.

3. On the front pushpin layers, use the bastard file and needle files to make the saw lines even and smooth.

4. Use the scribe to trace the back layer template onto pieces of the colored laminate (the middle pushpin layer). Saw out these traced shapes on the dotted line.

5. Using the template as a guide, drill a 2- to 3-mm hole in the center of the back pushpin layer. Commercial pushpins will go through these holes.

6. On the top pushpin layers, drill three holes with a 1-mm drill bit. Use the template as a guide for the placement of these holes.

7. Finish the front and back metal pushpin layers as desired. To achieve the pictured finish, hand-rub each metal layer in one direction with 220-grit sandpaper.

8. For each pushpin, use the snips to cut three 3- to 3.5-mm lengths of 18-gauge sterling silver wire. Sand the cut ends flat.

9. Thread the commercial pushpins through the hole in the back metal layers (see photo 1). Place one colored laminate piece on top of each commercial pushpin's head, and then position one top metal layer over the laminate. (This three-layer sandwich traps the commercial pushpin in place.)

10. While holding together one set of these layers with your fingers (you can tape them together if you wish), drill through the pushpin's top hole, using the previously drilled hole as a guide. Rivet this hole with a 3- to 3.5-mm length of the 18-gauge sterling silver wire. Repeat this process, drilling and riveting the pushpin's bottom hole. Finally, drill and rivet the hole in the center of the pushpin. Repeat this process for each pushpin.

11. Precisely following the top layer's contour, use the saw to cut off the extra edge of metal and colored laminate from each pushpin (see photo 2). File and sand the cut edges. Also sand off any burrs on the rivets.

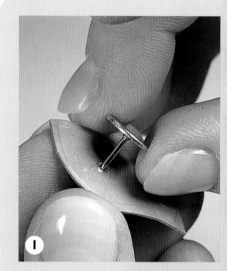

Curtain Tieback

For this gorgeous tieback, you'll use colored commercial rivets to attach multiple brass decorations to a gently curved aluminum strip.

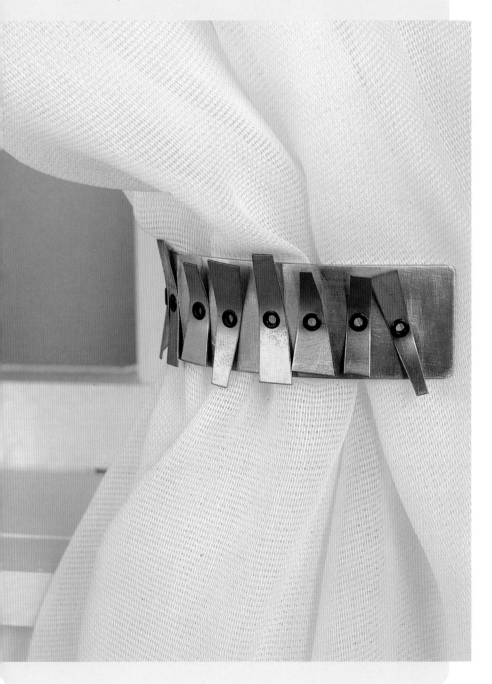

WHAT YOU NEED

Saw frame and blades

Aluminum sheet, 20 gauge

Needle files

Flexible shaft and accessories

Bastard file

Brass sheet, 24 gauge

Scribe

Center punch

Steel block

Chasing hammer

Drill bits

Colored commercial rivets*

Separators

Finishing tool or material of your choice

Flaring tool

Large round mandrel, approximately 2 inches (5 cm) in diameter

*You'll find these in the scrapbooking section of any major craft supply store, where they're often labeled as *eyelets*.

NOTE: Directions are for a single tieback. Repeat the steps to make more.

WHAT YOU DO

1. Use the saw to cut a 1¼ x 8-inch (3.2 x 20.3 cm) aluminum rectangle. File and sand the cut edges so they're even and snag-free. Round the corners of the rectangle with the bastard file.

2. Use the scribe to randomly mark slanted lines onto the brass, and then cut out 1½-inch (3.8 cm) irregularly shaped rectangles with the saw. Make sure none of the brass rectangles exceed ½ inch (1.3 cm) in width.

3. Dimple, and then drill a hole in each brass rectangle the same diameter as the commercial rivets. Place this hole in the center of each rectangle, or alter the hole position for an interesting effect.

4. Use the separators to draw a centerline down the length of the aluminum rectangle.

5. At one end of the rectangle, use the center punch to dimple two holes for drilling. Make one hole on the centerline 10 mm from the end, and dimple the second hole 20 mm from the end. (These holes will hold the screws that attach the curtain tieback to the wall.) Drill these holes with a 3-mm bit.

6. At the opposite end of the aluminum rectangle, dimple nine holes for drilling. Starting 15 mm in from the end of the rectangle, make each hole on the center-line and 15 mm apart. Drill these holes with a drill bit that corresponds to the size of the commercial rivets.

7. Sand all the metal to a 400-grit finish, and then finish the surface as desired. The matte finish on this project was achieved with a green kitchen scrub.

8. As shown in photo 1, rivet the irregular brass rectangles to the aluminum strips with the commercial rivets. These rivets are burgundy, but use any color you like.

9. Use your fingers to bend up the ends of the brass pieces, giving the curtain tieback added dimension.

10. Use your fingers to bend the curtain tieback around the round mandrel. Make the bend a little more than one-half the length of the tieback so that the end with the brass pieces is longer than the end with the drill holes. (This shape looks like a funny J from the side.) You can bend the metal to any shape you want as long as it holds back your curtains and looks pretty.

Twig Clock

Thin sticks mark the hours on this easy-to-assemble mixed-metal clock.

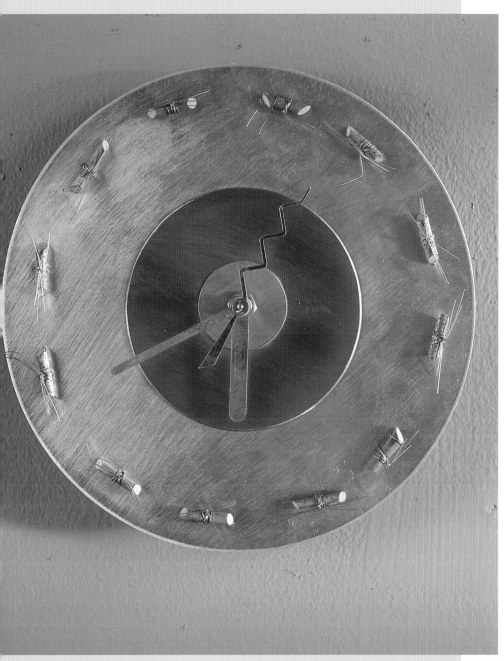

WHAT YOU NEED

Circle divider template

Scribe

Aluminum disc, 18 gauge, 7 inches (17.8 cm) in diameter

Copper disc, 24 gauge, 3 inches (7.6 cm) in diameter

Brass disc, 24 gauge, 1¼ inches (3.2 cm) in diameter

Center punch

Chasing hammer

Steel block

Flexible shaft and accessories

Drill bits

Separators

Thin sticks or found objects of your choice

Saw frame and blades

Commercial clockworks, including clock hands

Brass wire, 24 gauge

Finishing tool or material of your choice

Snips

Pliers (optional)

Epoxy

Battery for clock

WHAT YOU DO

1. Use the x-axis and y-axis lines on the circle divider template to find the center of each disc. Mark each point with the scribe. Dimple each mark with the center punch. Use a 1-mm bit to drill a hole at each dimple.

2. Open the separators to ½ inch (1.3 cm). Run them along the outside of the aluminum disc to create a line exactly ½ inch (1.3 cm) inside the disc's edge (see photo 1).

3. Using the circle divider template, mark 12 equally spaced points for the hours on the circle scribed in step 2. Dimple and drill each mark, using a 1-mm bit.

4. Use the saw to cut 12 pieces of the thin sticks, each ½ to ¾ inch (1.3 to 1.9 cm) long. Angle the stick ends if you want to add interest.

5. Snip three 3-inch (7.6 cm) lengths of 24-gauge brass wire for each stick for a total of 36 wire pieces. Using three wires at a time, wrap the wire around each stick. Twist the wire ends on top of the sticks as shown in photo 2 to form an attractive "package."

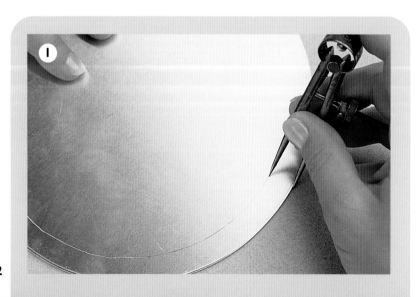

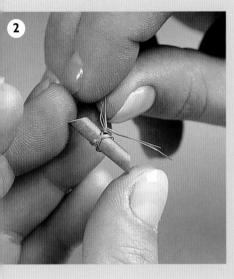
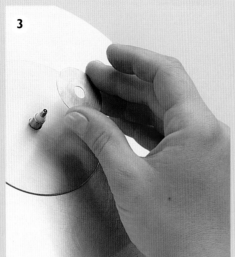
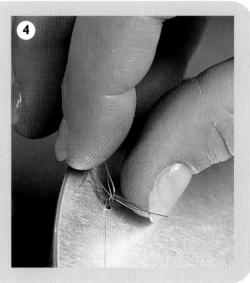

6. Measure the round fitting of the commercial clockworks. (This element will hold all three metal discs together.) Using the 1-mm hole predrilled in each disc as a guide, drill a new hole through the discs the same diameter as the clockwork's round fitting.

7. Give each metal disc a final finish. (These have been rubbed with a green kitchen scrub to produce a matte finish.)

8. Beginning with the large aluminum disc and ending with the small brass disc, thread each metal disc onto the commercial clockworks (see photo 3). Following the manufacturer's instructions, attach the clock hands.

9. Use the snips to cut 12 lengths of 24-gauge brass wire, each approximately 2 inches (5 cm) long. Attach the sticks to the clock by wrapping the 2-inch (5 cm) wires around the sticks several times, and then feeding the remaining wire ends through the 1-mm holes drilled in step 3. As shown in photo 4, use your fingers or pliers to twist the wire ends on the back side of the clock so the wire won't slip back through the hole, and then bend them over so they lie flat against the aluminum. Complete this step for all 12 sticks.

10. Follow the manufacturer's directions to mix the epoxy. Apply a small drop of epoxy to each twisted and bent wire on the back side of the aluminum disc. Let the epoxy dry. Place the battery in the clock, and set the time.

Shower Curtain Hangers

With their brightly colored commercial rivets, some functional and some strictly decorative, these stainless steel hangers are pure eye candy!

WHAT YOU NEED

Saw frame and blades

Steel ruler

Stainless steel sheet, 22 gauge

Needle files

Flexible shaft and accessories

Bastard file

Scribe

Circle divider template

Steel block

Center punch

Chasing hammer

Drill bits

Commercial rivets, colors of your choice*

Round mandrel or shower curtain rod

Flat-nose pliers (optional)

Finishing tool or material of your choice

*You'll find these in the scrapbooking section of any major craft supply store, where they're often labeled as *eyelets.*

NOTE: Directions are for a single shower curtain hanger. Repeat the steps to make more.

WHAT YOU DO

1. Use the saw to cut out a 1 x 1-inch (2.5 x 2.5 cm) stainless steel square. File or sand the cut edges straight. Round the corners if you want, or leave them at 90-degree angles.

2. Cut a strip of the stainless steel sheet 3½ to 4 inches (8.9 to 10.2 cm) long by ¼ inch (6 mm) wide. This will be the hook that hangs on the shower curtain rod. File or sand the cut edges straight.

3. Find the center of the 1 x 1-inch (2.5 x 2.5 cm) stainless steel square by drawing an X with the scribe from corner to corner. Use the circle divider template to find the x-axis and y-axis of the square, and mark these with the scribe. Measure ¼ inch (6 mm) in from each side, and mark these lines with the scribe. Dimple each line intersection, and then drill a hole the same diameter as the unflared end of the commercial rivets.

4. Place the narrow strip of stainless steel on top of the square in its center. Leave 3 inches (7.6 cm) of the strip hanging over one edge, and 1½ to 2 inches (3.8 to 5 cm) hanging over the opposite edge.

5. Mark a centerline down the length of the strip. Mark two drill holes on the strip's centerline at ¼-inch (6 mm) increments. (These marks correspond to the center hole on the middle row of the square and the center hole on the top row of the square.) Dimple and drill these holes.

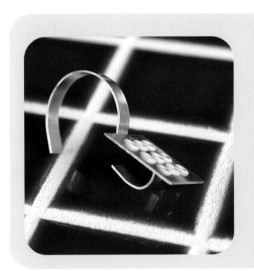

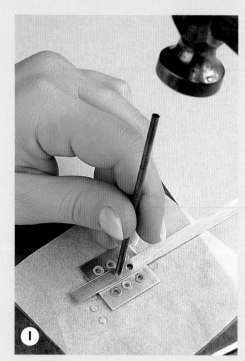

6. Except for the top two holes in the center column, rivet all the drilled holes with the commercial rivets. (These are all strictly decorative rivets.) Line up the drill holes in the stainless steel strip with the two unriveted holes. As shown in photo 1, rivet the strip onto the square with the commercial rivets.

7. Use your fingers to bend over the strip's long end toward the front of the shower curtain hanger. Wrap this length of the strip around the round mandrel as shown in photo 2. (You can even use your shower curtain rod as a mandrel to make an exact fit.) The hook should be springy from being work-hardened and snap right onto your shower curtain rod.

8. Use your fingers or the flat-nose pliers to pull up the strip's shorter end into a U shape (see photo 3). This section holds the curtain on the curtain hanger.

9. Finish the stainless steel as desired. These hangers feature the stainless steel's mill finish, which you can preserve if you're careful not to make any marks on the metal as you work.

Good Fortune Chopsticks

Set a splendid table with these vibrant acrylic and sterling silver chopsticks.

WHAT YOU NEED

Acrylic sheet, 1/8 inch (3 mm) thick, color of your choice

Saw frame and blades

Quick-drying epoxy*

Toothpick or small piece of wire

Square sterling silver wire, 4 mm

Bastard file

Needle files

Snips

Round sterling silver wire, 12 gauge

Flexible shaft and accessories

Chain-nose pliers

Rough-grit emery cloth

Clipboard

Drill bits

Fine-grit steel wool

*The label on your epoxy may claim a five-minute drying time, but this actually refers to the time it takes for the epoxy to *set*. The adhesive won't *dry* completely in those five minutes. To ensure the most secure bond, let the epoxy dry overnight.

NOTE: Directions are for two chopsticks. Repeat the steps to make more.

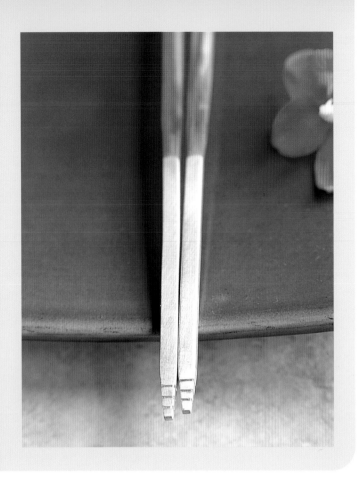

WHAT YOU DO

1. Cut four strips of the acrylic sheet, each ³⁄16 x 5 inches (.5 x 12.7 cm). Follow the manufacturer's instructions to mix the epoxy. Using a toothpick or a small piece of wire, spread a thin layer of epoxy on one side of each strip of acrylic. Join two strips together, with their glued sides facing. Repeat for the remaining two strips. Let the epoxy dry overnight.

2. Measure and saw two pieces of the 4-mm square sterling silver wire, each 3 inches (7.6 cm) long.

3. As shown in photo 1, use the bastard file to taper one end of each piece of the square wire cut in step 2. Begin filing the taper about ½ inch (1.3 cm) in from the end. Keep filing away metal until you create a chopstick tip that's a 2-mm square.

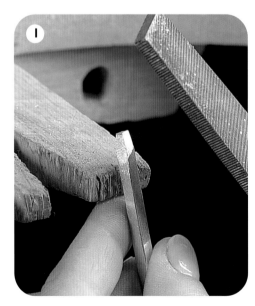

4. Use the needle files to decorate the tapered metal chopstick tips (see photo 2). Experiment with various needle files to create interesting effects. (In this example, a triangular needle file was used to carve parallel lines.)

5. On the opposite, untapered end of the silver wire, use the barrette needle file to carve the metal into a peg that's approximately ¼ inch (6 mm) long and 2 mm in diameter (see photo 3). This peg will later join the silver to the acrylic. Make one peg on each piece of square silver wire.

6. Use the snips to cut a piece of the 12-gauge round sterling silver wire, approximately 2 inches (5 cm) long. Round the cut wire ends with 400-grit sandpaper. Hold one end of the wire in the chain-nose pliers, and gently turn the wire to make a flat spiral shape. As shown in photo 4, bend ¼ inch (6 mm) of the spiral's end perpendicular to the curve so it rests centered on the end of the chopstick.

7. File and sand the glued acrylic into even and square ³⁄₁₆ x 5-inch (.5 x 12.7 cm) strips. To sand straight and even lines, first use a piece of rough-grit emery cloth on a clipboard, and then follow with 220- and 400-grit sandpaper.

8. Using a 2-mm bit, drill approximately 5 mm into the center of both ends of each acrylic piece. You'll attach the metal to the acrylic in these holes.

9. Follow the manufacturer's instructions to mix the epoxy. Use a toothpick or small piece of wire to place a drop of epoxy into each hole in the acrylic pieces. Insert one metal chopstick end and one wire spiral into each acrylic piece. Rest the chopsticks on a flat table with the metal and acrylic parts aligned. Let the epoxy dry overnight.

10. File and sand the bottom chopstick joints so the acrylic tapers into the silver end. Rub the chopsticks with a fine-grit steel wool for a final finish.

High-Flying Journal

This stunning stainless steel and acrylic blank book is the perfect place to write a journal, craft a poem, or sketch a scene.

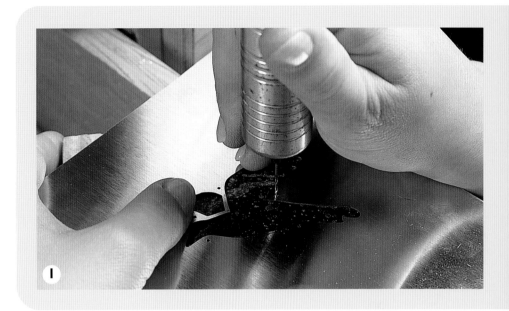

WHAT YOU NEED

Saw frame and blades

Stainless steel sheet, 22 gauge

Bastard file

Flexible shaft and accessories

Graphite transfer paper

Scribe

Photocopied template, page 118

Steel block

Center punch

Chasing hammer

Drill bits

Needle files

Snips (optional)

**Round sterling silver wire,
18 gauge**

**Plastic laminate sample, color of
your choice***

Journal paper of your choice**

Plastic coil binder**

Permanent marker

Chain-nose pliers

*Ask for free samples at your local
home improvement center.

**Purchase plastic coil binders and jour-
nal paper at full-service copy shops and
office supply stores. You can make the
journal as thick as you want, as long as
there's a spiral binding large enough to
hold the paper. Your local full-service
copy shop or office supply store will
often stock many different sizes.

WHAT YOU DO

1. Use the saw to cut out two 5 × 6-
inch (12.7 × 15.2 cm) rectangles from
the stainless steel sheet. Round the rectangle corners with the bastard file. Sand
the rectangle edges with 220-grit sandpaper as needed to remove all burrs.

2. Use the graphite paper to transfer the
bird design from the photocopied template onto one of the 5 × 6-inch (12.7 ×
15.2 cm) stainless steel rectangles. Pierce
and saw out the design. File the saw lines
to remove all burrs and snags.

3. Dimple, and then use the 1-mm bit to
drill the five rivet holes shown on the
photocopied template. The rivet holes
are strategically placed on the metal
around the bird design to firmly and
evenly hold the laminate in place.

4. Use the snips or the saw to cut five
pieces of the 18-gauge round sterling
silver wire, each approximately 3.5 to 4
mm long. File or sand the cut ends flat
and even.

5. Place the colored laminate sample
under the cut-out bird design. As shown
in photo 1, use one of the holes drilled
in the stainless steel as a guide to drill a
hole through the laminate. Using a piece
of the wire cut in step 4, rivet together
the laminate and stainless steel through
this hole.

6. Reposition the colored laminate as
needed. Directly across from the rivet
made in step 5, drill a second hole
through the laminate, using a hole drilled
in the stainless steel as a guide. Rivet
together both layers with a piece of the
sterling silver wire. Repeat this process to
drill and rivet all remaining holes.

7. Take the journal paper to your local full-service copy shop or office supply center, where an automated paper cutting machine can cut your stack of paper to a specific size. Have the paper cut to 5¾ x 4¾ inches (14.6 x 12.1 cm). This leaves a nice ¼-inch (6 mm) stainless steel barrier around the paper to keep its edges neat.

8. While at the copy shop or office supply center, have holes made down one edge of the paper to accommodate the spiral binding. (They may charge a nominal fee for this service, but it's well worth the expense. The journal won't open and close smoothly with uneven holes, so it's best to have them professionally made.) Bring home the prepared journal paper.

9. Using a piece of the journal paper as your guide, mark the locations for drilling the holes on the stainless steel front and back covers. Use a permanent marker to trace the holes, and then dimple each hole's center with the center punch and chasing hammer (see photo 2).

10. Drill the dimpled holes with the 4-mm bit. (You may need to start with a smaller drill bit for each hole, and then go back and enlarge the hole.) File off any burrs, and then sand the drilled holes to a 400-grit finish. Make as few marks as possible on the stainless steel sheet to preserve the metal's attractive mill finish.

11. To bind the journal's edge, thread the plastic coil through the holes in the decorative front cover, the paper, and then the back cover. Leave the coil ends approximately 4 mm longer than the top and bottom of the bound journal. As shown in photo 3, use the chain-nose pliers to bend under the extra length of coil to secure it in place and make the ends smooth.

62

Falling Leaf Fan Pull

With its animated design and artfully sawed accents, this aluminium and acrylic fan pull is a favorite in every season.

WHAT YOU NEED

Graphite transfer paper

Scribe

Photocopied templates, page 118*

Aluminum sheet, 22 gauge

Saw frame and blades

Center punch

Steel block

Chasing hammer

Needle files

Flexible shaft and accessories

Green kitchen scrub or finishing material of your choice (for aluminum)

Acrylic sheet, 1/8 inch (3 mm) thick

Fine-grit steel wool or finishing tool or material of your choice (for acrylic)

Drill bits

Aluminum tubing, 2.5-mm OD, 1.5-mm ID

Flaring tool

Snips

Sterling silver wire, 18 gauge

Chain-nose pliers

Small bead, approximately 5 to 10 mm in diameter

Round mandrel, 5 mm in diameter

Ball-chain connector**

*You can create your own fan-pull design if you wish. Just make sure to include space near the top of the acrylic layer for a hole through which you'll attach the pull to the fan pull's wire loop.

**Ball-chain connectors are small parts used by jewelers and beaders. You can purchase them from any jewelry supplier or bead store.

63

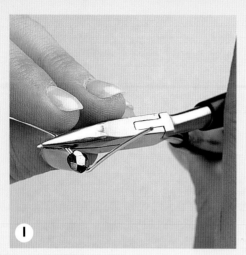

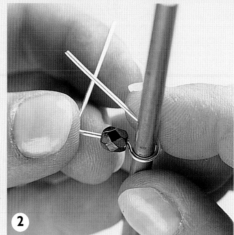

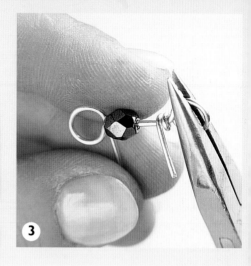

WHAT YOU DO

1. Use the graphite transfer paper to trace design A from the photocopied template (or your own design) onto the aluminum sheet. Trace the design twice: once for the front side of the fan pull, and once for the back side.

2. Pierce and saw out the aluminum design. File and sand all the cut edges so they're smooth and snag-free. Sand each metal surface as well, and finish as desired. (This aluminum was rubbed with a green kitchen scrub to produce a matte finish.)

3. Use the graphite transfer paper to trace design B from the photocopied template (or your own design) onto the acrylic sheet.

4. Slowly and evenly saw out the traced acrylic shape. (If you saw too quickly, the acrylic will melt onto the saw blade and break the blade.) File and sand the edges of the acrylic piece. (To give the acrylic a matte finish, this piece was rubbed with a fine-grit steel wool.)

5. On one layer of the aluminum, use the center punch to dimple four points for drilling the rivet holes. Center these points down the length of the aluminum

and space them approximately ⅜ inch (9.5 mm) apart. Drill each dimple with a 2.5-mm bit.

6. Center the drilled aluminum layer on top of the acrylic layer. Center the bottom, undrilled aluminum layer under the acrylic. Tape together all three layers to secure them in place.

7. Use the saw to cut four pieces of the 2.5-mm aluminum tubing, each approximately 7 mm long. Sand the ends of the cut tubing.

8. Using the top hole on the top aluminum layer as a guide, drill through the acrylic and the bottom aluminum layer with a 2.5-mm bit. Thread one piece of the 7-mm tubing through this hole, and rivet.

9. Using the bottom hole on the top aluminum layer as a guide, drill through the acrylic and the bottom aluminum layer with a 2.5-mm bit. Thread one piece of the 7-mm tubing through this hole, and rivet. Repeat this process to drill and rivet the last two holes.

10. At the point marked on template design B, use a 1.25-mm bit to drill a hole

through the acrylic layer. The wire hook for the fan's chain will be inserted through this hole.

11. Use the snips to cut a 2-inch (5 cm) length of the 18-gauge sterling silver wire. Hold the wire with the chain-nose pliers approximately ¾ inch (1.9 cm) in from one end. Bend the wire at a 90-degree angle. Thread the bead onto the opposite, unbent wire end. Hold this end with the pliers about ¾ inch (1.9 cm) in from the end. Bend the wire end at a 90-degree angle in the opposite direction as shown in photo 1.

12. While holding the wire on one side of the bead, wrap the wire tail around the 5-mm round mandrel (see photo 2). Repeat this wrap on the other side of the bead. Thread one end of the wire through the hole drilled in the acrylic and the other end through the ring on the ball-chain connector.

13. While firmly holding the wire circle with the chain-nose pliers, use your fingers to wrap the wire's tail three times around the flat part of the wire next to the bead (see photo 3). Repeat this wrapping technique on the opposite side of the bead. Use the snips to trim off any extra wire.

Pearl & Silver Napkin Rings

*Adorn sterling silver with delicate dimple chasing and a sewn border
of pearls to create these glamorous napkin rings.*

WHAT YOU NEED

Saw frame and blades

Sterling silver sheet, 24 gauge

Flexible shaft and accessories

Needle files

Bastard file

Scribe

Steel ruler

Center punch

Steel block

Chasing hammer

Chasing tools (optional)

Drill bits

**Sterling silver tubing, 1.9-mm
OD, 1.2-mm ID**

Flaring tool

**Round mandrel, approximately
1 inch (2.5 cm) in diameter**

Rawhide or wooden mallet

Fine silver wire, 24 gauge

Pliers

Pearls or beads, 5 to 6 mm

NOTE: Directions are for a single
napkin ring. Repeat the steps to
make more.

4. On the marked lines nearest the silver rectangle's edges, drill holes with a .75-mm bit at each dimple in ¼-inch (6 mm) increments. These are the holes for threading the fine silver wire and pearls or beads. The remaining dimples are simply decorative accents.

5. Draw one line ⅛ inch (3 mm) in from each end of the rectangle. (These lines are perpendicular to those drawn in step 2.) Dimple these lines at the centerline and ⅛ inch (3 mm) in from the top and bottom edges of the rectangle. Drill holes at the dimples using a 1.9-mm bit.

Vertical lines drawn in step 2

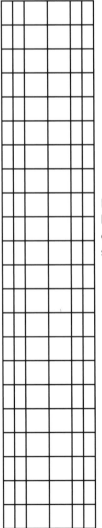

Horizontal lines drawn in step 3

WHAT YOU DO

1. Use the saw to cut a 5½ x 1-inch (14 x 2.5 cm) rectangle from the 24-gauge sterling silver sheet. File or sand the cut edges so they're completely straight, and then round the corners with the bastard file.

2. Use the scribe and the steel ruler to draw lines that are ⅛ inch (3 mm) and ¼ inch (6 mm) in from each of the silver rectangle's long edges. Draw a centerline down the rectangle that's ½ inch (1.3 cm) in from both edges. As shown in figure 1, you'll have drawn a total of five parallel lines.

3. Starting at one end of the silver rectangle, mark each parallel line at ¼-inch (6 mm) increments (also shown in figure 1). Use the center punch as a chasing tool to dimple each of these marks (see photo 1) or decorate the napkin ring with any chasing tool you like.

Figure 1

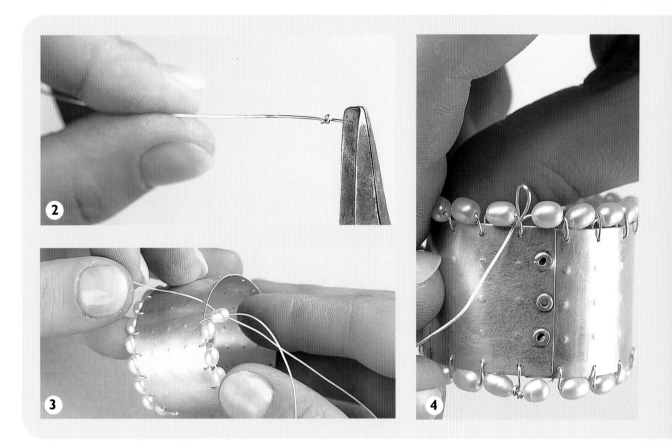

6. Saw three pieces of tubing, each about 4 mm long. Sand the edges flat. Using the flaring tool and chasing hammer, flare one side of each piece of tubing. Make sure to tap lightly on the tubing while it's resting on the steel block.

7. Bend the silver rectangle into a ring with the dimples and line marks on the inside. Line up the drilled holes for the tube rivets. One at a time, insert the flared tubing into the holes, with the flared end on the inside of the ring. Place the ring on the round mandrel, and rivet. Repeat this process to rivet each flared tube. If the drilled holes don't perfectly match, you can re-drill the holes as long as the flare of the tube rivet covers the new, larger hole.

8. Place the napkin ring on the round mandrel. Use the rawhide or wooden mallet to gently hammer the ring into a perfect circle. As shown in this example, the dimple decoration is very subtle from the back side. You could create a more prominent decoration if you wish.

9. Cut a piece of the 24-gauge fine silver wire, approximately 15 inches (38.1 cm) long. Tie a knot in one end of the wire. To make a tight knot, hold the wire with the pliers in one hand, and, with your other hand, firmly pull the knot into place (see photo 2).

10. Thread the wire into a hole near the napkin ring's seam, making sure the knot is on the inside of the ring. Add one pearl or bead to the wire, and then

thread the wire through the next hole in the napkin ring. (This action is similar to sewing.) Position the pearl or bead so it rests on top of the metal in a manner that appeals to you. Continue sewing with the wire and adding individual pearls or beads all the way around the napkin ring until you reach your starting point. To complete the sewing, wrap the end of the wire around the initial loop several times .

11. As shown in photo 3, repeat step 10 on the opposite edge of the napkin ring. To complete the sewing, wrap the end of the wire around the initial loop several times (see photo 4). Give the ring a final finish. (This one is rubbed with a fine-grit steel wool. A black patina would also look great on this piece.)

67

Mission-Style Towel Bar

This tasteful towel bar mixes the refined fashion of pierced, sawed, and chased copper with ordinary hardware supplies.

WHAT YOU NEED

Saw frame and blades

Copper sheet, 18 gauge

Needle files

Bastard file

Scribe

Metal ruler

Dividers

Steel block

Center punch

Chasing hammer

Flexible shaft and accessories

Drill bits

Chasing tool of your choice

Finishing tool or material of your choice

Wooden or rawhide mallet

Vise (optional)

Scrap leather or copper sheet (optional)

Copper tubing, ½ inch (1.3 cm) in diameter, 2 feet (60.9 cm) long*

Copper end caps, ½ inch (1.3 cm) in diameter**

*You can purchase a precut length of copper tubing, or you can use the saw to cut the tube to any length you want.

**A copper end cap is a piece of commercial hardware you can buy at your local home improvement center.

WHAT YOU DO

1. Use the saw to cut out two 3 × 2½-inch (7.6 × 6.4 cm) rectangles from the 18-gauge copper sheet. File the cut edges straight, and round the corners with the bastard file.

2. On the 3-inch (7.6 cm) side of each piece cut out in step 1, draw a line 2 inches (5 cm) inside the edge to make a 2 × 2½-inch (5 × 6.4 cm) rectangle. (The spare 1 × 2½-inch [2.5 × 6.4 cm] copper rectangle will become the wall mount for the towel bar.)

3. From corner to corner, draw an X inside each marked 2 × 2½-inch (5 × 6.4 cm) copper rectangle to find its center point. Use the dividers to draw a ½-inch (1.3 cm) circle in the center of the rectangle.

4. Draw additional lines on both sides and 2.5 mm outside of the X lines drawn in step 3. Use the dividers to mark a second circle 5 mm outside of the ½-inch (1.3 cm) circle drawn in step 3. Make sure the smallest circle is ½-inch (1.3 cm) in diameter.

5. Pierce and saw out the shaded areas shown in figure 1. File the cut edges straight.

6. For hanging the towel bar on the wall, use a 3.5-mm bit to drill two screw holes on the 1 × 2½-inch (2.5 × 6.4 cm) rectangle. Drill these holes on the centerline of the rectangle's length and ¾ inch (1.9 cm) in from each edge.

7. Decorate both sides of the remaining copper surface with whatever chasing tool you want. This example features marks made with a tool carved into an O design.

8. Sand the copper to a 400-grit finish, and then give it any additional final finish you desire.

9. Use the steel block to bend the 1 × 2½-inch (2.5 × 6.4 cm) copper rectangle to a 90-degree angle. Use your fingers to push the metal over, and then use the rawhide or wooden mallet to create a good 90-degree angle. (You may need to hang the edge of the steel block off your worktable to accommodate the width of the rectangle as it bends.)

OPTION: As shown in photo 1, you could also place the copper rectangle in a vise to bend the metal. Cover the jaws of the vise to protect the metal surface, and then position the decorative side of the towel bar hanger in the vise jaws. Make sure the smaller rectangle with the screw holes is free of the vise so you can bend it.

10. Clean up any hammer marks from the copper's surface. Insert one end of the ½-inch (1.3 cm) copper tubing into each of the sawed end-holes. Place one copper end cap on each end of the tubing (see photo 2). Screw the towel bar into the wall.

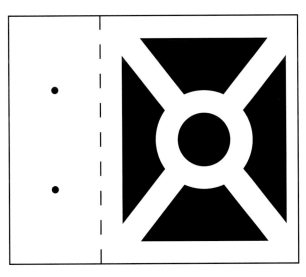

Figure 1

Whimsical Wall Hook

This silver and acrylic charmer is sure to make you smile. Why not make several foot-hooks for a funky and functional installation?

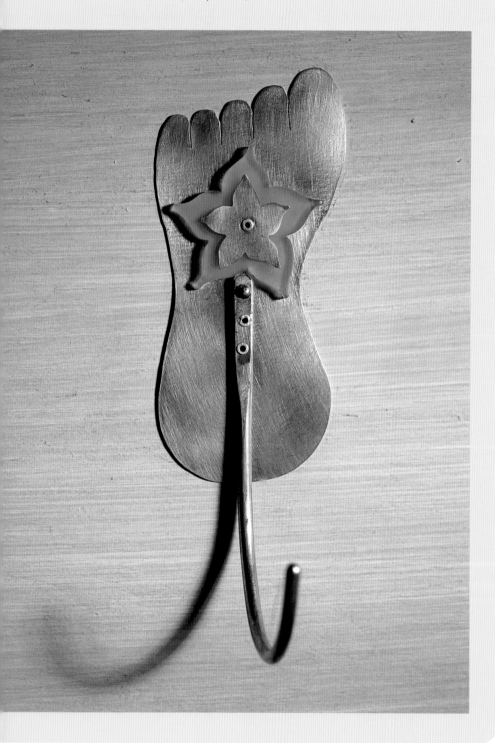

WHAT YOU NEED

Graphite transfer paper

Photocopied templates, page 119

Scribe

Nickel silver sheet, 24 gauge

Saw frame and blades

Needle files

Bastard file

Flexible shaft and accessories

Acrylic sheet, ⅛ inch (3 mm) thick color of your choice

Steel or nickel wire, 8 gauge

Metal ruler

Chasing hammer

Steel block

Center punch

Drill bits

Finishing tool or material of your choice

Round mandrel, 2 inches (5 cm) in diameter (optional)

Rawhide or wooden mallet (optional)

Sterling silver tubing, 2.6-mm OD, 1.9-mm ID

Flaring tool

WHAT YOU DO

1. Use the graphite paper to transfer photocopied templates A and B (the foot and the small lotus flower) onto the nickel silver sheet. Saw out these shapes, and then file and sand the cut edges.

2. Using the graphite paper and photocopied template C, transfer the large lotus flower onto the acrylic sheet. Saw out this shape. File and sand the cut edges.

3. Cut a 5-inch-long (12.7 cm) piece of the 8-gauge steel or nickel wire. (You should use your saw to cut heavier gauge wires.) As shown in photo 1, flatten a 1-inch (2.5 cm) section of one of the wire's ends with the ball side of the chasing hammer. Remember to hammer on top of the steel block for resistance. Round both ends of the wire with a file so the hook won't snag.

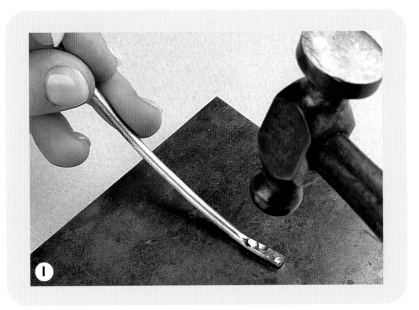

4. Dimple the flat part of the wire in three places, each 5 mm apart and 5 mm away from the edge. Drill these holes with a 2.6-mm bit. The bottom two holes are for riveting the wire to the metal foot, and the top hole is for screwing the hook into the wall.

5. Drill the holes for attaching the lotus flower to the foot. Dimple and drill the center of the small metal lotus flower with a 2.6-mm bit. Repeat this process on the large acrylic flower. Position the flowers on top of the foot. Use the scribe to mark the hole through the flowers and onto the foot. Dimple and drill the foot at this marked point.

6. File and sand all cut pieces to a 400-grit finish, and then give the pieces a final finish. You can achieve this particular finish with a fine-grit steel wool.

7. Curve the end of the 8-gauge wire to make a J-shaped hook (see photo 2). You can bend the wire with your hands or with a rawhide or wooden mallet and a mandrel. If it's not somewhat hardened already, bending the wire will help give it strength. The bent wire should be hard enough to safely support anything you want to hang.

8. Use the saw to cut two pieces of the 2.6-mm sterling silver tubing, each 4 to 5 mm long. Sand the cut ends with 220-grit sandpaper.

9. Use the saw to cut one 6-mm-long piece of the 2.6-mm sterling silver tubing. Sand the cut ends with 220-grit sandpaper. This is the tube rivet that attaches the lotus flower to the foot.

10. Thread the 6-mm tube rivet through the foot, the acrylic flower, and the small metal flower. Rivet together these elements.

11. Position the flattened end of the hook on top of the foot and directly under the base of the lotus flower. Use the scribe to mark the middle drilled hole onto the foot. Dimple, and then drill at this marked point with a 2.6-mm bit. Rivet the hook to the foot.

12. Repeat the process in step 11 to mark, dimple, drill, and rivet the bottom hole on the flat part of the hook.

13. Mark, dimple, and drill the top hole on the flat part of the hook. Leave it rivet-free so you can screw the hook into the wall through this opening.

Modern Mirror

Three curvy layers of aluminum and acrylic hold a round mirror in place to form this freestanding tabletop accessory.

WHAT YOU NEED

Graphite transfer paper

Photocopied templates, page 120

Aluminum sheet, 18 gauge

Saw frame and blades

Bastard file

Needle files

Flexible shaft and accessories

Acrylic sheet, ⅛ inch (3 mm) thick, color of your choice

Circle divider template

Scribe

Long metal ruler (optional)

Dividers

Steel block

Chasing hammer

Center punch

Drill bits

Finishing tool or material of your choice

Acrylic mirror sheet, ⅛ inch (3 mm) thick

Clear tape

Aluminum tubing, 2.5-mm OD, 1.6-mm ID

Flaring tool

73

WHAT YOU DO

1. Use graphite paper to transfer photo-copied template A (the mirror's rear metal layer) onto the aluminum sheet. Use the saw to cut out this shape. File and sand the edges smooth.

2. Use graphite paper to transfer photo-copied template B (the mirror's middle layer) onto the acrylic sheet. Use the saw to cut out this shape. File or sand the cut acrylic edges smooth.

3. Use graphite paper to transfer photo-copied template C (the mirror's front layer) onto the aluminum sheet. Use the saw to cut out this shape. File or sand the cut edges smooth.

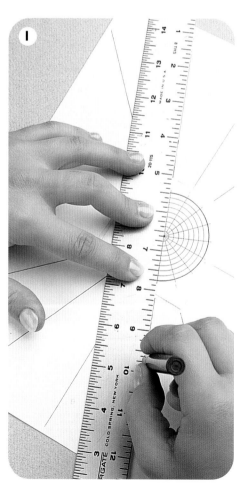

4. Use the circle divider template to find the x-axis and the y-axis of the acrylic layer. Mark the center point with the scribe. (If your circle divider template isn't large enough, use a ruler to extend the lines of the template onto a piece of paper as shown in photo 1. Lay the acrylic layer on top of the paper instead of on the circle divider template.)

5. Use the dividers to scribe a circle onto the acrylic layer, approximately ¾ to 1 inch (1.9 to 2.5 cm) inside its edge. Pierce and saw out this interior circle.

6. Repeat step 5 on the front (smallest) aluminum layer.

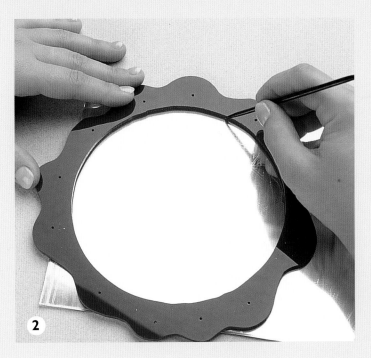

2

3

4

7. Give each layer a final finish. In this example, the aluminum was rubbed with a green kitchen scrub for a matte finish. To preserve the acrylic's original shiny finish, you must work with care. Rubbing the acrylic with a fine-grit steel wool produces a matte finish.

8. Use the pierced and sawed acrylic layer as a template for marking the size of the acrylic mirror. Lay the acrylic layer on top of the acrylic mirror, remembering to conserve space on the mirror sheet. As shown in photo 2, use the scribe to trace the inner circle. Pierce, and then saw out this circle. It should fit nicely into the acrylic layer.

9. Cover the acrylic mirror with paper to prevent scratching. Arrange all the mirror layers on top of each other, with the acrylic mirror in place. Use clear tape to secure the layers.

10. Cut 12 pieces of aluminum tubing, each approximately 6 to 7 mm long. Sand the cut ends flat.

11. Drill a 1.65-mm hole in the center of one of the scalloped curves. The hole should pass through the aluminum and acrylic layers, but not through the acrylic mirror. (The mirror is trapped in place by the top layer and the bottom layer.) Rivet through this drilled hole using a piece of the 6- to 7-mm tubing cut in step 10.

12. Realign the mirror layers as needed, and then drill a second hole directly across from the hole made in step 11. Tube rivet through this hole. As shown in photo 3, continue drilling and riveting using the "clock" method described on page 27 of The Basics section.

13. To create the stand, gently bend back the neck and the base of the mirror (see photo 4). Curve the neck to give it flexibility and balance. When you set the mirror on a table, adjust the bend in the neck for stability and to create the proper viewing angle.

Classic Pen Holder

Alternating tubes of copper and brass elevate the humble pen holder to the level of a distinguished desk accessory.

WHAT YOU NEED

Separators

Steel ruler

Copper sheet, 24 gauge

Saw frame and blades

Steel block

Center punch

Chasing hammer

Flexible shaft and accessories

Drill bits

Needle files

Bastard file

Circle divider template

Scribe

Finishing tool or material of your choice

Brass tubing, four 12-inch-long (30.5 cm) pieces, 3.25-mm OD, 2.5-mm ID

Copper tubing, seven 12-inch-long (30.5 cm) pieces, 3.25-mm OD, 2.5-mm ID

Brass tubing, eight 12-inch-long (30.5 cm) pieces, 2.25-mm OD, 1.75-mm ID

Flaring tool

Clear acrylic spray (optional)

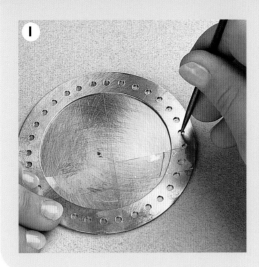

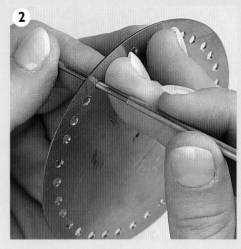

WHAT YOU DO

1. Open the separators to 1¾ inches (4.4 cm). Draw two circles on the 24-gauge copper sheet, making sure to conserve space on the metal.

2. Close the separators to 1¼ inches (3.2 cm). Place one point of the separators on the center mark of one of the circles drawn in step 1. Draw a second, smaller circle inside the first circle. Saw out both large copper circles. After dimpling, pierce and saw out the interior circle drawn on one metal disc to make a large copper "washer." File the outer edges of both discs smooth. File the inner edge of the washer.

3. Open the separators to ¼ inch (6 mm). Using the outside edge of the copper washer as a guide, draw a centerline around the washer with the separators. Place the washer on the circle divider template, and use the scribe to divide the washer into 16 equally spaced sections.

4. Use your eye to determine the center point between each of the 16 sections marked on the copper washer. Scribe a new line between each to make a total of 32 sections on the circle. Dimple each section mark on the centerline of the washer. Use a 1-mm bit to drill a hole at each dimple.

5. Place the copper washer on top of the 3½-inch (8.9 cm) disc. Tape together the two pieces of metal to ensure they don't move. As shown in photo 1, push the scribe through the washer's drilled holes to mark the positions to be drilled on the bottom disc. Remove the tape, and then drill all 32 holes on the bottom copper disc with the 1-mm bit. Sand the disc and the washer with 400-grit sandpaper, and then finish as desired. (These were finished with a fine-grit steel wool.)

6. Using the 1-mm drilled holes as a guide, re-drill all holes in the copper washer and in the copper disc with a 2.25-mm bit. (You're enlarging the holes to accommodate the 2.25-mm tubing.)

7. Use the saw to cut the 3.25-mm OD brass tubing into 12 sections, each 3¾ inches (9.5 cm) long. Use the saw to cut the 3.25-mm OD copper tubing into 20 sections, each 3¾ inches (9.5 cm) long. Sand the cut tubing ends with 400-grit sandpaper.

8. Use the saw to cut 32 pieces of the 2.25-mm OD brass tubing, each 4 inches (10.2 cm) long. Sand the cut ends flat with 220-grit sandpaper. (These tubing pieces are longer so they can pass through the thickness of the washer and the disc and become the flared part of the tube rivet.)

9. Feed one of the 4-inch (10.2 cm) brass tubing pieces through one hole in the bottom copper disc. As shown in photo 2, thread one of the 3¾-inch (9.5 cm) pieces of brass tubing onto the thinner tubing. Feed the opposite end of the 4-inch (10.2 cm) brass tubing piece through one hole in the washer. Rivet.

10. Carefully plan the decorative placement of the brass and copper tubing. This project uses a sequence of three brass tubing pieces separated by five copper tubing pieces. To make sure you place the correct type of tube in the right location, use a pencil to mark their places on the copper washer.

11. Repeat step 9 to rivet all holes following the "clock method" described on page 27 of The Basics section. Using this method ensures even rivets and proper rivet strength. (If you have any trouble lining up the holes, it's perfectly fine to redrill holes, as long as the flared rivet covers the larger opening.)

12. Finish the pen holder as desired. (A fine-grit steel wool was used on this example.) Seal the pen holder with a clear acrylic spray, or leave the metal open to naturally develop a patina.

Mail-Call Sorter

Freestyle cut-out designs reveal a burst of acrylic color, making this contemporary aluminum accessory a dazzling addition to any home.

WHAT YOU NEED

Scribe

Long metal ruler

Aluminum sheet, 18 gauge

Saw frame and blades

Needle files

Bastard file

Acrylic sheet, ⅛ inch (3 mm) thick, color of your choice

220-grit sandpaper (optional)

Flexible shaft and accessories

Photocopied templates, page 121

Graphite transfer paper

Steel block

Center punch

Chasing hammer

Drill bits

Finishing tool or material of your choice

Aluminum tubing, 2.7-mm OD, 2-mm ID

Flaring tool

Vise

Scrap leather or copper sheet

WHAT YOU DO

1. Use the scribe to mark three 5½ × 5-inch (14 × 12.7 cm) rectangles on the aluminum sheet. Saw out these rectangles, file their edges straight, and lightly round each corner with the bastard file.

2. Use the scribe to mark three 4¾ × 4 ¾-inch (12.1 × 12.1 cm) squares on the acrylic sheet. Saw out these acrylic squares, and use the bastard file to file their edges straight. (If you want even smoother edges, you can run the acrylic along a piece of 220-grit sandpaper.)

3. Measure and mark two 1 × 16-inch (2.5 × 40.6 cm) strips on the aluminum sheet. Saw out these strips, and then file or sand their edges straight. Round the corners with the bastard file.

4. To decorate the aluminum rectangles, use the piercing and sawing designs from the photocopied templates, or create your own shapes. Use the graphite transfer paper to transfer the designs onto the aluminum, and then pierce and saw them out. Use the needle files to smooth any uneven saw lines. To further tidy up the sawed-out designs, you can sand them with 220-grit sandpaper. Give each aluminum rectangle a final finish. (These were rubbed in circles with a fresh piece of 220-grit sandpaper.)

5. Refer to the templates for the placement of the drill holes. Mark these points on the aluminum rectangles, dimple them with the center punch, and then drill the holes with a 2.75-mm bit. Four of the drill holes are for attaching the aluminum to the acrylic, and two of the holes are for attaching the aluminum and acrylic to the aluminum strips.

6. Use the saw to cut 12 pieces of the aluminum tubing, each 7 to 8 mm long. Sand the cut ends flat with 220-grit sandpaper. These tube rivets will attach the acrylic to the aluminum rectangles.

7. Place an acrylic piece on one of the rectangles. As shown in photo 1, line up the acrylic so three of its edges are approximately ⅛ inch (3 mm) inside the aluminum, and the fourth acrylic edge is approximately ¾ inch (1.9 cm) inside the aluminum. (You can tape the acrylic to the aluminum to secure this placement if you like.) Use the holes previously drilled in the aluminum as a guide for drilling the holes in the acrylic. Drill two holes at opposite corners, and then rivet together the acrylic and aluminum. Drill the remaining two opposite holes, and complete the riveting. Repeat this step twice to rivet together the remaining acrylic pieces and aluminum rectangles.

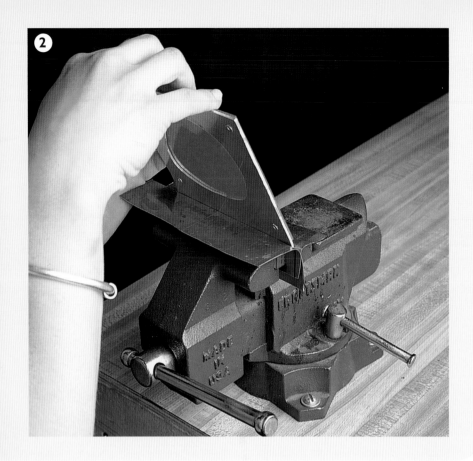

②

8. To protect the aluminum from scratches and mars, cover the jaws of the vise with a scrap of leather or copper sheet. Evenly place one aluminum and acrylic rectangle into the vise with only 1 inch (2.5 cm) of the metal in the jaws. Tighten the jaws of the vise. With the acrylic side of the rectangle facing away from you, use your fingers to gently bend the aluminum toward you to create a 45-degree angle (see photo 2). Repeat this step to bend the remaining two rectangles of riveted aluminum and acrylic.

9. Draw a line 10 mm inside one edge of both aluminum strips cut in step 3. Measure and mark points on this line 1 inch (2.5 cm), 6 inches (15.2 cm), and 11 inches (27.9 cm) in from one end of each strip. Dimple, and then drill a hole at each point with a bit the same diameter as the aluminum tubing. You'll later use these holes to rivet the aluminum and acrylic rectangles to the strips.

10. Draw the centerline down the length of each aluminum strip. Measure and mark points on the centerline ½ inch (1.3 cm) in from each strip end. Dimple and drill holes at these points that are the same diameter as the aluminum tubing. You'll later use these holes to screw the mail holder onto the wall.

11. Cut six pieces of the aluminum tubing, each 5 to 6 mm long. Sand the cut edges flat. Starting at the top of the mail sorter, rivet the aluminum and acrylic rectangle to the strips. Next, rivet the middle rectangle, and finally the bottom rectangle, onto the strips. Screw the mail holder onto the wall.

Sparkling Salad Servers

Gorgeous details like the serene fish design and the delicately sewn handles make this set of gently domed salad servers truly spectacular.

81

WHAT YOU DO

1. Open the separators to 1½ inches (3.8 cm). Use them to mark two 3-inch (7.6 cm) circles on the stainless steel sheet. Saw out the circles, and then file the cut edges with the bastard file.

2. Use the graphite paper to transfer the fish design from the photocopied templates onto the stainless steel circles. Also transfer the outline of the fork-shaped teeth onto one circle.

3. Pierce and saw out the fish design and saw out the fork-shaped teeth. Use the needle files and the bastard file to file all cut edges smooth.

4. Transfer the placement marks for the drill holes onto each stainless steel circle. (You'll use these holes to rivet the handles to the circles.) Dimple these marks, and then drill the holes with a 1.45-mm bit.

5. Place one stainless steel circle into the large wooden dapping block. Using the wooden dap and the chasing hammer, gently dap the circle into a dome as shown in photo 1. To create an even dome, begin dapping around the circle's edges, and then move into the center. Repeat this process to dome the second circle.

6. Use the saw to cut two 15-inch (38.1 cm) lengths of the 12-gauge brass wire. Use the chasing hammer to flatten the wire ends until they're each approximately 5 mm wide (see photo 2). Flatten only the last ¼ to ⅜ inch (6 to 9.5 mm) of wire on each end.

7. Bend the center of the 12-gauge wire pieces around the ¼- to ½-inch (.6 to 1.3 cm) round mandrel. To make sure the wire bends in the center, mark the middle of the piece with a pencil. Place the

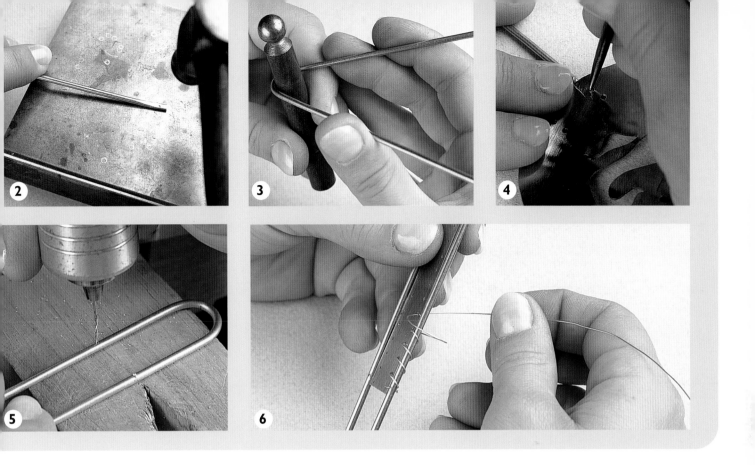

mark on the round mandrel. As shown in photo 3, use your fingers to slowly and equally bend the wire around the mandrel, one side at a time. Make sure the flattened wire ends are parallel.

8. Use the saw to cut two pieces of the 22-gauge stainless steel sheet, each ½ x 2½ inches (1.3 x 6.4 cm). File or sand the cut edges straight and even. Use the separators to draw a line 3 mm in from the longer edges of both rectangles. Mark these lines at 5-mm increments. Dimple each mark, and then use a .5-mm bit to drill a hole at each dimple.

9. Place the flattened ends of the bent brass wire under the rivet holes drilled in the stainless steel circles. Using the holes as a guide, mark the brass wire ends with a scribe (see photo 4). Dimple the top two marks. Use a 1.45-mm bit to drill the top two holes on both of the bent brass wire handles.

10. Use the saw to cut eight pieces of 16-gauge round brass wire, each approximately 5 mm long. Sand the cut wire ends flat.

11. Use the 5-mm pieces of the 16-gauge brass wire to rivet together the top two holes of one circle and one handle. Once connected, use the existing pair of lower holes as your guide to drill through the circle and the flattened ends of wire with a 1.45-mm bit. Use 5-mm pieces of the 16-gauge brass wire to rivet together the lower holes.

12. Use the center punch to dimple two marks on one handle's arms, each approximately 1 inch (2.5 cm) inside the curve of the wire handle. Use a .5-mm bit to drill holes at these dimples (see photo 5). Drill the holes perpendicular to the length of the handle. Repeat this step on the second handle.

13. Cut a 6-inch (15.2 cm) length of the 22-gauge brass wire. Knot the wire at one end. (For tips on knotting wire, refer to step 9 of the Pearl & Silver Napkin Ring instructions on page 67.) From the back side of the handle, thread the wire through one hole drilled in step 12. Pull the end wire until the knot rests against the back of the handle. Sew the ½ x 2½-inch (1.2 x 6.4 cm) rectangle to the handle by threading the wire through the drilled holes, and then wrapping it around the handle as shown in photo 6. When you reach the last hole, knot the wire end on the back of the stainless steel rectangle. Repeat this sewing step on the opposite side of the rectangle and then on the second handle.

14. Finish the salad servers as you like. This pair was finished with a white bristle disc on a flexible shaft machine to produce a slick finish on the stainless steel.

Howl-at-the-Moon Lampshade

This scenic lampshade features frisky copper pups and brilliant

brass moons riveted onto a cylinder of aluminum flashing.

WHAT YOU NEED

Shears

Aluminum flashing*

Photocopied templates, page 123

Graphite transfer paper

Brass sheet, 24 gauge

Copper sheet, 24 gauge

Saw frame and blades

Steel block

Center punch

Chasing hammer

Flexible shaft and accessories

Drill bits

Needle files

Finishing tool or material of your choice

Masking tape

Round clip-on lampshade frame, 5 inches (12.7 cm) in diameter**

Aluminum tubing, 3.25-mm OD, 2.5-mm ID

Round mandrel

Flaring tool

Aluminum tubing, 2.5-mm OD, 1.5-mm ID

Lamp base, to fit lampshade

Lightbulb

*You can buy this material at the home improvement center or hardware store.

**You can remove the clip-on frame from an old lampshade, or purchase a new one from a craft supply store or home improvement center.

WHAT YOU DO

1. Use the shears to cut the aluminum flashing into a 10 × 17½-inch (25.4 × 44.5 cm) rectangle. Round the corners of the rectangle with the shears.

2. Beginning at the end of one 17½-inch (44.5 cm) side of the rectangle, use the shears to cut 12 equally spaced tabs, each ½ × ½ inch (1.3 × 1.3 cm) large and 1 inch (2.5 cm) apart (see photo 1). You'll later use these tabs to attach the lampshade to the frame.

3. Use the graphite paper to transfer the moon designs from the photocopied templates onto the 24-gauge brass sheet. Transfer the dog designs from the photocopied templates onto the 24-gauge copper sheet. Pierce and saw out these designs. At the location indicated on each template, use a 2.5-mm bit to drill a hole on each dog and each moon piece. File the cut edges and sand each piece to a 400-grit finish. Give all dog and moon pieces a final finish. (These were rubbed in a circular motion with 220-grit sandpaper.)

4. Using a 4-mm bit, drill random holes in the aluminum flashing. These holes represent stars in the sky, and allow light to pass through the shade when the lamp is illuminated.

5. Use a pencil and a ruler to draw a straight line ½ inch (1.3 cm) inside one of the flashing rectangle's 10-inch (25.4 cm) edges. Beginning ½ inch (1.3 cm) in from one corner, mark nine points on this line, each 1-inch (2.5 cm) apart. Drill each marked point with a 3.25-mm bit.

6. Bend the 17-inch (44.5 cm) side of the aluminum flashing rectangle into a circle. Overlap the ends of the circle by 1 inch (2.5 cm). Use masking tape to hold the circle in this position. As shown in photo 2, insert the round lampshade frame into the top of the circle and make sure it fits. (If the fit isn't perfect, it's better for the aluminum circle to be a little larger than the frame.) If necessary, adjust the aluminum so the frame fits inside, and then re-close the circle with tape.

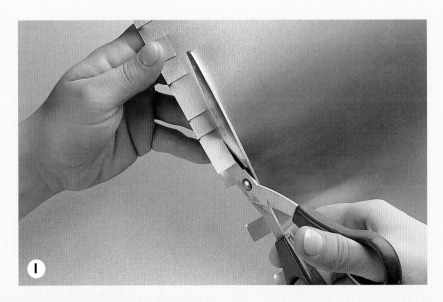

1

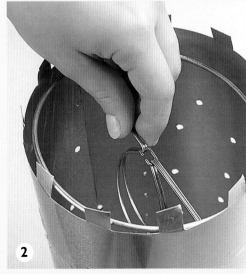

2

7. Using the nine holes drilled in step 5 as a guide, drill holes through the bottom layer of the overlapped metal with a 3.25-mm bit.

8. Use the saw to cut nine ¼-inch (6 mm) lengths of the 3.25-mm aluminum tubing. Sand the cut ends flat. On one end of each piece of cut tubing, saw two perpendicular 3-mm slits. (For detailed slitting instructions, refer to step 4 of the Candle Snuffer on page 88.) Bend the ends of the slit tubing open to make a flared "flower" shape.

9. One at a time, insert the flared tubing into the nine holes drilled in the over-lapped aluminum circle. Position the flared part of the tubing on the inside of the circle. As you rest the aluminum circle on the round mandrel for resist-ance, use the flaring tool to flare the exterior tubing ends, and then rivet all nine holes as shown in photo 3. Remove the tape from the aluminum circle.

10. Decide where you want to position the dogs and the moons on the lamp-shade. You can space them evenly around the lampshade or place them closer together so they all can be viewed from one side. Using a 2.5-mm bit, drill a hole in the shade for each dog and each moon shape.

11. Use the saw to cut six 8-mm lengths of the 2.5-mm aluminum tubing to use as rivets. Sand the cut ends of the rivets flat. Cut six 4-mm lengths of the 3.25-mm aluminum tubing to use as spacers. Sand the cut ends of the spacers flat.

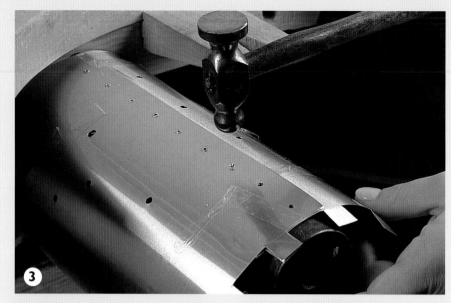

3

4

5

12. Make two perpendicular 3-mm slits in one end of each of the 8-mm-long tube rivets. Bend back the slits into a flared "flower" shape. One at a time, with the flared end inside the lampshade, insert the tube rivets into the holes drilled in step 10. Thread one spacer tube on top of each of the tube rivets. Using the round mandrel for resistance, position one cut-out dog or moon on the appropriate spacer, and rivet (see photo 4). Repeat this process to attach all dogs and moons to the shade.

13. Assemble the lamp base, lightbulb, and frame. Slide the lampshade over the frame. As shown in photo 5, use your fingers to gently fold the lampshade tabs over the frame, securing the lampshade in place. (Don't bend the metal tabs back and forth. Aluminum flashing work hardens quickly, and the tabs could break off.)

Candle Snuffer

*This sophisticated snuffer features a brass cone with flared
sterling silver rivets and a twisted-wire handle.*

WHAT YOU NEED

Photocopied template, page 122

Brass sheet, 24 gauge

Saw frame and blades

Needle files

Chain-nose pliers (optional)

Flexible shaft and accessories

Scribe

Center punch

Chasing hammer

Drill bits

**Sterling silver tubing, 1.9-mm OD,
1.25-mm ID**

Round-nose pliers

**Round mandrel or tapered round
mandrel**

Wooden or rawhide mallet

**Finishing tool or material
of your choice**

Round brass wire, 14 gauge

**Small round mandrel,
approximately ¼ inch (6 mm)
in diameter**

Regular drill

**Round sterling silver wire,
18 gauge**

Snips

WHAT YOU DO

1. Use the photocopied template to trace the snuffer shape onto the brass sheet. Saw out the traced form. File and sand the cut edges.

2. Use the scribe to mark a line 5 mm in from one edge of the sawed brass form. Use the center punch to make three dimples on this marked line: 10 mm, 25 mm, and 40 mm in from the snuffer form's curved edge. Use a 1-mm bit to drill a hole at each dimple.

3. Use your fingers to bend the metal into a cone shape. To allow plenty of room for riveting, overlap the ends approximately 7 to 8 mm. (At this point, don't worry if the metal doesn't look like a perfect cone.)

4. Use the saw to cut three pieces of the sterling silver tubing, each approximately 8 mm long. Sand the cut tubing ends. Hold the saw frame so its blade meets one open end of one piece of tubing at a 90-degree angle. Saw into the tubing, making a 3- to 4-mm slit (see photo 1). Turn the tubing 90 degrees, and saw another slit into its opening, again 3 to 4 mm long. Repeat this process to make perpendicular slits in one end of the remaining pieces of cut tubing. Use your fingers or chain-nose pliers to gently flare out the slotted tubing ends like a flower. Set these flared tubes aside.

5. Firmly hold the overlapped ends of the cone in place, and drill through the existing 1-mm holes with a 1.9-mm bit. (This bit is the same size as the sterling silver tubing.) With the flared end on the inside of the cone, thread a piece of the prepared tubing through the top cone hole. With the drill hole holding the tubing in place, repeat the process used in step 4 to saw slits on the opposite end of the threaded tubing. Flare out the newly slit ends. Repeat this process for the remaining drilled holes and tubing pieces.

6. Place the cone on the round or tapered round mandrel. (It's fine if the mandrel isn't exactly cone-shaped; just use one side of the mandrel for resistance in hammering.) As shown in photo 2, gently hammer the cone into shape with the rawhide or wooden mallet. Use light hammer blows, and repeatedly turn the cone around on the mandrel. Always hammer from the top, making sure to move the cone around the mandrel, not the hammer around the cone. Also hammer the flared rivets to secure. Your hammering will fasten the rivets without harming them.

7. Drill two holes through the top of the cone on opposite sides. Make these holes approximately 3 mm in from the cone's top edge and approximately 3 mm in diameter.

8. Sand the cone and give it a final finish. The matte finish on this snuffer was created by rubbing a green kitchen scrub in one direction on the metal.

9. Cut a 30-inch (76.2 cm) length of the 14-gauge brass wire. Use your fingers to gently bend the wire in half without making a sharp crease in the middle. To make sure the wire stays round at the bend, place the small mandrel inside the curve.

10. Place the cut ends of the bent brass wire into the chuck of the drill. Firmly tighten the chuck to secure the wire in the clamps of the drill. Replace the mandrel in the bend of the wire. Hold the wire horizontally in front of you with the mandrel out to one side and the drill out to the other side. Turn on the drill and let the wire twist together as shown in photo 3. (This project features a medium tight twist. You can twist the wire more tightly or more loosely as long as it holds its position.) Let the wire "snap back," or untwist, by removing the mandrel from the wire before removing the wire from the drill.

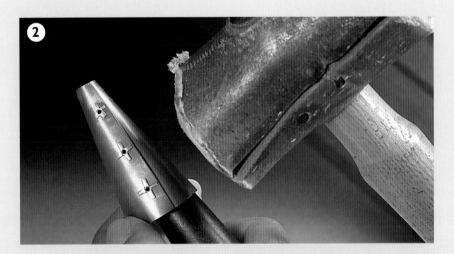

11. Cut a 30-inch (76.2 cm) length of the 18-gauge sterling silver wire. Thread the wire through the circle in the bent end of the twisted brass wire. Center the sterling silver wire, so you'll have plenty to wrap around the brass twist. As shown in photo 4, loop the sterling silver wire around the circle of brass wire three or four times.

12. Twist the sterling silver wire down the entire length of the brass twisted wire, carefully placing it between the brass wire twists (see photo 5). Snip the sterling silver wire ends even with the twisted brass wire ends.

13. Untwist approximately 10 mm of both wire ends. Open them into a V shape. As shown in photo 6, use the round-nose pliers to curve up the wire ends. (Each arm of the V is made of two wires, one brass and one silver. Work with these two wires as one element, holding them both together in the round-nose pliers instead of bending them one at a time.)

14. Thread one arm of the wire V into the top hole of the metal cone from the inside. Use the round-nose pliers to squeeze together the V, allowing the second arm of the V to fit into the opposite hole in the cone top. (Because it's springy from being work-hardened, the second arm of the V should easily snap into place.)

15. Rub the twisted wires with a green kitchen scrub for a final finish. Sand the wire ends in the top of the cone with 400-grit sandpaper.

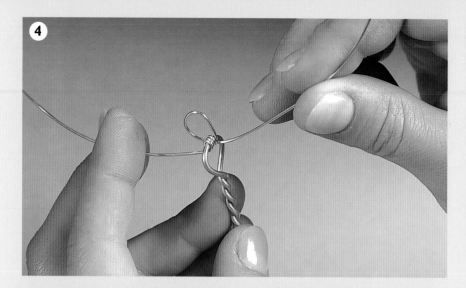

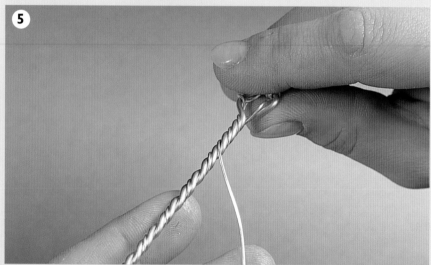

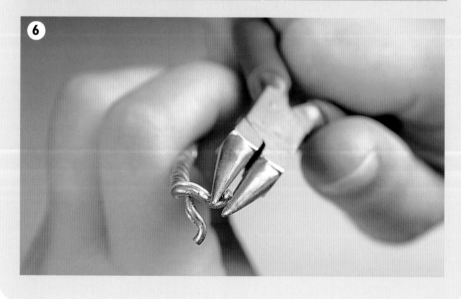

Red-Hot Spatula

Whether you're flipping pancakes on the griddle or burgers on the grill, do it in style with this acrylic and stainless steel spatula.

WHAT YOU NEED

Graphite transfer paper

Photocopied templates, page 124

Stainless steel sheet, 20 gauge

Saw frame and blades

Steel block

Center punch

Chasing hammer

Flexible shaft and accessories

Drill bits

Bastard file

Needle files

Vise

Scrap leather or copper sheet

Flat stainless steel rod, $1/8$ x $1/4$ inch (3 mm x 6 mm), approximately 10 inches (25.4 cm) long

Red acrylic sheet, $1/8$ inch (3 mm) thick

Clear acrylic sheet, $1/8$ inch (3 mm) thick

Round brass wire, 16 gauge

Brass tubing, 3.25-mm OD, 2.25-mm ID

Flaring tool

Epoxy resin (optional)

Fine-grit steel wool (optional)

Finishing tool or material of your choice

WHAT YOU DO

1. Use graphite paper to transfer the design for the flat end of the spatula from the photocopied template onto the stainless steel sheet. Saw out the spatula shape, and then pierce and saw out the flame design. File the outside edges of the spatula with the bastard file and the inside edges of the flames with the needle files. Slightly round the corners of any sharp areas.

2. Use a 1.45-mm bit to drill two holes on the narrow end of the spatula at the positions shown on the template.

3. Cover the jaws of the vise with scrap leather or copper sheet to prevent any teeth marks from damaging the metal. Put ½ inch (1.3 cm) of one end of the 10-inch-long (25.4 cm) stainless steel rod into the jaws of the vise. Firmly tighten the jaws. As shown in photo 1, bend the rod toward you, forming a 30-degree angle, and then remove the rod from the vise.

4. Use the graphite paper to transfer the shape of the oval handle from the photocopied template onto the red acrylic sheet. Saw out this oval shape. Using it as a template, trace the acrylic oval two additional times on the red acrylic sheet and two times on the clear acrylic sheet (see photo 2). Saw out all the traced ovals. (You don't need to file the edges of the ovals.)

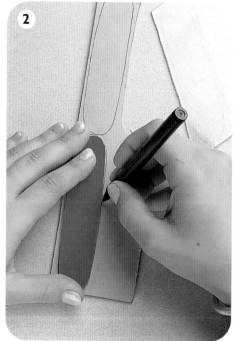

5. Use the saw to cut two pieces of the 16-gauge round brass wire, each approximately 5 mm long. Sand the cut edges flat.

6. Place the bent end of the stainless steel rod on top of the two holes in the narrow end of the spatula. From the bottom of the spatula, use the scribe and a drilled hole as a guide to mark one hole on the bent end of the rod. Dimple, and then drill this hole through the rod with a 1.45-mm bit.

7. Thread one piece of the 5-mm round brass wire through the matching spatula and rod holes, and rivet.

8. Using the second hole on the spatula as a guide, use a 1.45-mm bit to drill through the stainless steel rod. Rivet together the spatula and the rod through this hole.

9. Lay the opposite end of the flat rod on top of one red acrylic oval. Center the end of the rod lengthwise on the oval, about 3 inches (7.6 cm) away from the oval's end. Trace the rod's shape onto the acrylic oval (see photo 3). Use the saw to carefully cut out the shape, precisely following the traced lines as shown in photo 4. The flat rod should fit perfectly into the sawed-out space.

10. Use the saw to cut eight pieces of the brass tubing, each approximately 17 to 18 mm long. Sand the cut ends flat.

11. Use the photocopied handle template to find and mark the y-axis of one complete red acrylic oval. Mark eight points on the y-axis line, each ½ inch (1.3 cm) apart and ½ inch (⅓ cm) in from each end as shown on the handle template. Use a 3.25-mm bit to drill a hole at each of these marks.

12. Starting with the drilled red oval as the top layer, align the acrylic ovals on top of each other. Place a clear oval between each red one and the sawed oval in the center. Using the first hole of the spatula handle's top end as a guide, drill through all four layers of acrylic with a 3.25-mm bit. Using the brass tubing cut in step 10, rivet together all the acrylic layers through this hole.

13. Following the method described in step 12, drill and rivet the fifth hole down from the top end of the spatula handle (see photo 5).

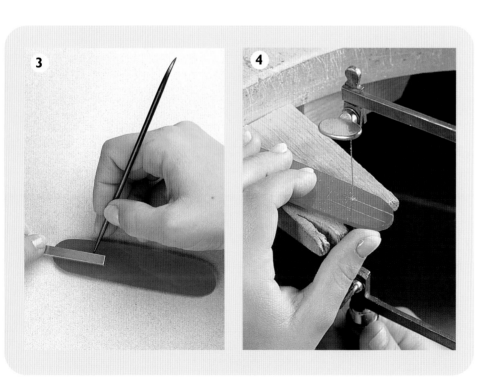

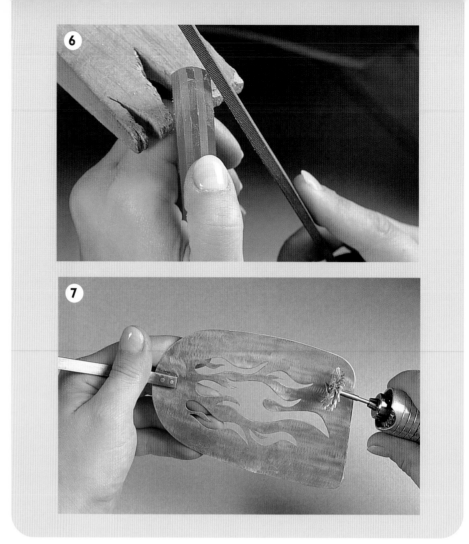

14. Firmly hold together the acrylic layers with your fingers. As shown in photo 6, use the bastard file to round the end of the spatula handle where the stainless steel rod will be inserted. (This will be a time-consuming filing process, but hang in there! If you have a belt sander, the work will go much quicker.) Acting as if the acrylic were one whole piece instead of several layers, round its end into a perfect oval shape. File the top and bottom edges of the acrylic to a gently sloping angle.

OPTION: You can use epoxy resin to glue together the acrylic layers, and then rivet the layers and file their edges round. (Refer to step 1 of the Good Fortune Chopsticks on page 58 for further instructions.)

15. Insert the handle end of the stainless steel rod into the slot in the middle acrylic layer. Using the hole at the bottom end of the spatula handle as a guide, drill through the acrylic layers and the stainless steel rod. Rivet this hole with the brass tubing cut in step 10.

Now that the handle is firmly in place, continue drilling through the holes and riveting together the layers until all are complete.

16. Use the bastard file to finish rounding the edges of the spatula handle. File as much as you like to achieve the desired curve, and then use 220-grit sandpaper to smooth the edges and remove all file marks. Sand the handle

again, this time with 400-grit paper to smooth out the marks from the previous sanding. Rub the handle with fine-grit steel wool to shine the acrylic.

17. Give the metal parts of the spatula a final finish. On this example, a white bristle disc was used on the flexible shaft to create an interesting surface (see photo 7).

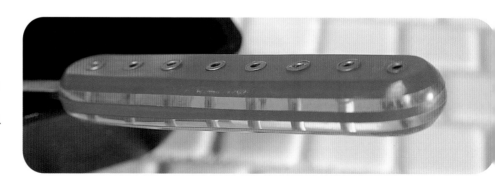

Candle Chandelier

Sleek copper strips support hammered brass candleholders to form this distinctive chandelier.

5. Use the saw to cut out four discs from the 24-gauge brass sheet. Make each disc 3 inches (7.6 cm) in diameter. File the cut edges so the discs are perfectly round. Find the center of each disc by placing it on the circle divider template and drawing its x-axis and y-axis with a pencil. Dimple the center of each disc for drilling.

6. Place one brass disc on the wooden dapping block. Use the wooden dap and the chasing hammer to press the disc into the largest depression on the dapping block. Crinkle the edges of the disc as you force the metal into the depression as shown in photo 2. Keep dapping until the disc edges are crinkled to your liking. Repeat this step on all remaining brass discs.

WHAT YOU DO

1. Use the saw to cut out two strips of the 18-gauge copper sheet, each 12 x 2 inches (30.5 x 5 cm). File or sand the cut edges straight, and then gently round the corners with the bastard file.

2. Saw a slot down the center of each copper strip. Make one slot 4 inches (10.2 cm) long for strip A, and one slot 8 inches (20.3 cm) long for strip B. The slots must be precisely 1 mm wide to accommodate the thickness of the 18-gauge copper sheet.

3. Saw another slot at the opposite end of copper strip A. Make this slot 3½ inches (8.9 cm) long and precisely 1 mm wide.

4. Place one copper strip on the steel block. Use the chasing hammer to tap the strip's edges on both sides, giving the metal a hammered texture (see photo 1). Repeat this step for the second copper strip.

2

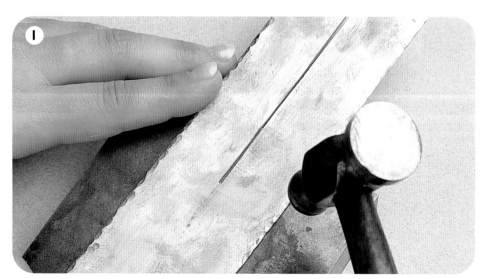

7. Use a 2.25-mm bit to drill the center holes of the discs dimpled in step 5. Give each domed and crinkled disc a final finish. (These have been rubbed with a fine-grit steel wool.)

8. On copper strips A and B, use a 2.25-mm bit to drill holes at the positions indicated in figure 1, letter a. Give both copper strips a final finish. (These were rubbed with a fine-grit steel wool.)

9. On the opposite ends of copper strips A and B, use a 2.25-mm bit to drill centered holes ½-inch (1.3 cm) in from the ends (see figure 1, letter b for hole placement).

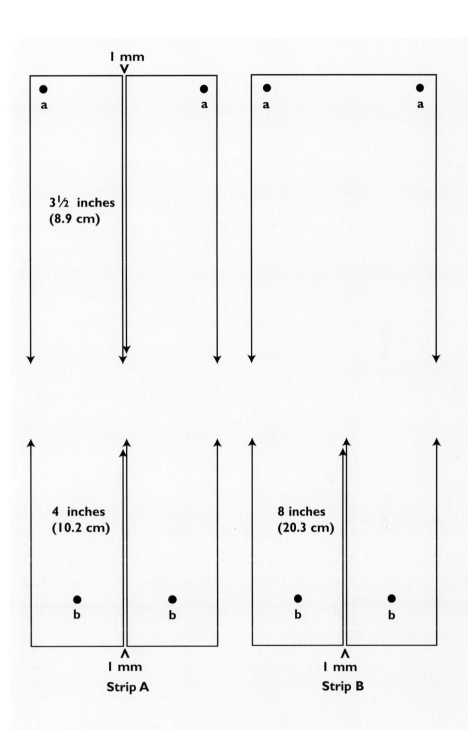

Figure 1

10. Insert the 4-inch (10.2 cm) slot in copper strip A into the 8-inch slot in strip B. The strips should intersect at the top in the form of a cross. Use your fingers to bend the ends of each strip in opposite directions. Start by bending the ends of one strip in opposite directions, and then bend the ends of the second strip under those bent first (see photo 3). These bends secure the strips in their cross position.

11. Use a 2.25-mm bit to drill a centered hole through both copper strips where they overlap.

12. Use the saw to cut six 5- to 6-mm pieces of the brass tubing. Sand the cut ends flat. Insert one tubing piece into each of the two holes drilled in step 11, and rivet.

13. Insert one piece of the cut tubing through the drilled hole on one domed brass disc. Thread this piece of tubing through one of the holes drilled in step 9 on the bent end of the copper strip. Rivet the domed disc to the strip. Repeat this step to rivet the remaining brass discs to the bent copper strips.

14. Use the snips to cut the brass ball chain in half, making two 15-inch (38.1 cm) lengths. (You can use a longer or shorter chain, depending on where you want to hang your chandelier.) Thread each length through two adjacent holes at the top of the candle chandelier. Connect the ends of the ball chain with the brass ball-chain connectors as shown in photo 4. Hang the candle chandelier from a brass hook screwed into the ceiling.

Nouveau Picture Frame

With simple cold-connecting skills you can create a dramatic metal frame to give your prized photographs the presentation they deserve.

WHAT YOU NEED

Saw frame and blades

Stainless steel sheet, 22 gauge

Bastard file

Needle files

Flexible shaft and accessories

Clear acrylic sheet, ⅛ inch (3 mm) thick

Steel block

Center punch

Chasing hammer

Drill bits

Graphite transfer paper

Photocopied template, page 125

Copper sheet, 24 gauge

Chasing tool of your choice (optional)

Finishing tool or material of your choice

Copper tubing, 2.25-mm OD, 1.7-mm ID

Copper tubing, 1.7-mm OD, .6-mm ID

Flaring tool

Vise

Scrap leather or copper sheet

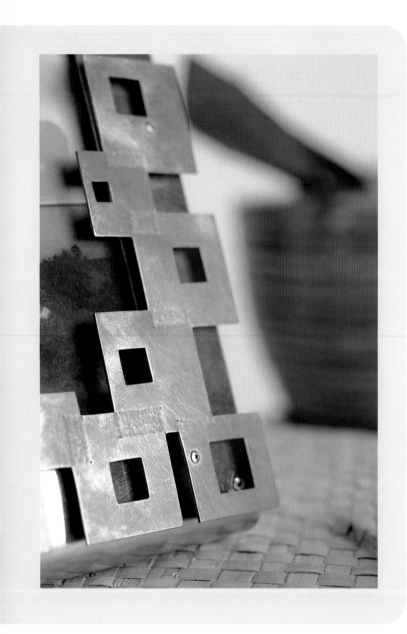

WHAT YOU DO

1. Use the saw to cut a 4½ x 8-inch (11.4 x 20.3 cm) stainless steel rectangle for the front layer of the frame. File or sand the cut edges straight and even.

2. Use the saw to cut a 4½ x 6-inch (11.4 x 15.2 cm) stainless steel rectangle for the back layer of the frame. Use the saw to cut a 4½ x 6-inch (11.4 x 15.2 cm) piece of clear acrylic for the frame's middle layer. File or sand all edges straight and even. Place the acrylic aside in a safe place where it won't get scratched. (If the clear acrylic is coated with a layer of thin plastic, leave it on until you rivet together the frame.)

3. On the front stainless steel frame layer, measure and mark an interior rectangle 1 inch (2.5 cm) in from the top and the side edges, and 3 inches (7.6 cm) up from the bottom edge. These marked lines form a 4 x 2½-inch (10.2 x 6.4 cm) rectangle for the frame's picture opening. Pierce and saw out this rectangle. File the cut edges straight.

4. On the back stainless steel frame layer, measure and mark an interior rectangle 1 inch (2.5 cm) in from the top and side edges and 4 inches (10.2 cm) up from the bottom edge. Pierce and saw out this rectangle. This opening allows you to slide pictures in and out of the frame.

5. Use graphite transfer paper to transfer the photocopied design template onto the 24-gauge copper sheet. Pierce and saw out this decorative copper element. File all cut edges smooth and straight. Chase designs on the copper if you wish. (On this example, a matting tool was used at the overlaps of the squares to more clearly identify their borders.) If you wish, you can also give the copper element a patina.

6. Give both the front and back stainless steel picture frame layers a final finish. (In this example, the mill finish was left on the stainless steel.) Finish the decorative copper element. (This one was rubbed with fine-grit steel wool.)

7. Cut seven 3-mm-long pieces of the 2.25-mm OD copper tubing. Sand the cut ends flat. Cut 10 pieces of the 1.7-mm OD copper tubing, each 8 mm long. Sand the cut ends flat. Put the cut tubing pieces aside in a safe place.

8. Measure and mark lines 5 mm in from each edge of the back stainless steel frame layer. Dimple the points where the marked lines intersect at each of the four corners as shown in photo 1. Using the 1-mm bit, drill a hole at each dimple.

9. Use the drilled holes on the back frame layer as a guide for the placement of the holes on the front frame layer. Lay the back frame layer on top of the front frame layer, and align their top edges. (The frame opening on the front layer will be partially covered by the back layer.) Push the scribe through each of the drilled holes, and mark their placement on the top frame layer. Dimple and drill the holes on the top frame layer.

10. Place the decorative copper element in position on top of the frame. Decide where you want to place the rivets to secure the decoration to the frame. (If you've used the design from the template, also use its marks to guide the rivet placement.) Use at least three rivets to ensure a good hold. Mark and drill these locations on both the front frame layer and on the decorative copper element.

11. Line up the top edge of the clear acrylic piece with the top edge of the frame's front layer. Lay the decorative copper element on top of the front frame layer and the acrylic layer. With a 1.7-mm bit and using the drill holes on the decorative copper element as a guide, drill through the front and the acrylic frame layers.

12. Thread one smaller tubing piece through the acrylic frame layer and the front frame layers. Place a piece of the larger tubing on the smaller tubing to act as a spacer. Thread the remainder of the smaller tubing through the drilled hole in the copper element (see photo 2), and rivet. (Be extremely careful when hammering to flare the rivet on the acrylic. Use firm but not overly forceful hammer blows. A blow that's too heavy could crack the acrylic.) Repeat this step to fully rivet the copper element to the acrylic frame layer and the front frame layer.

13. Align the back frame layer with the acrylic and the front frame layer. Using the holes drilled in steps 8 and 9 as a guide, redrill one corner hole with a 1.7-mm drill bit. Thread one piece of the smaller tubing through the frame's front and acrylic layers. Place a piece of the larger tubing onto the smaller tubing to act as a spacer. Thread the remainder of the smaller tubing through the back frame layer, as shown in photo 3, and rivet.

14. Following the sequence shown in figure 3 on page 27 of The Basics section, repeat step 13 to drill and rivet the diagonally opposite predrilled hole. Use the same technique to rivet the frame's final two predrilled holes.

15. Cover the teeth on the vise with scrap leather or copper. Place the bottom 2 inches (5 cm) of the frame's front layer in the vise, leaving a little room (about ¼ to ½ inch [.6 to 1.3 cm]) to make the bend. With the top of the frame facing you, gently push the frame over the jaws of the vise until you make a 90-degree bend (see photo 4). Remove the frame from the vise and continue bending the top of the frame away from you until the frame is balanced and stands on its own.

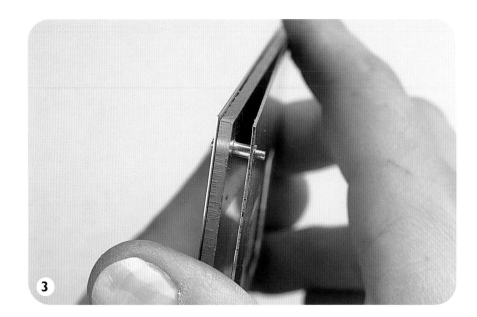

The Gallery

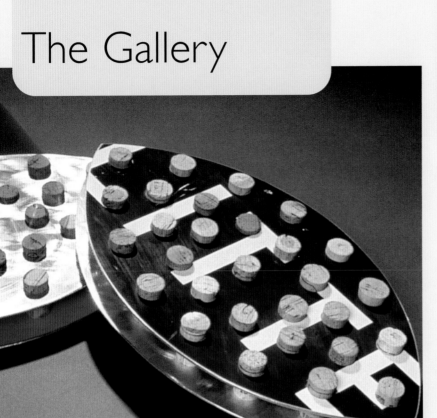

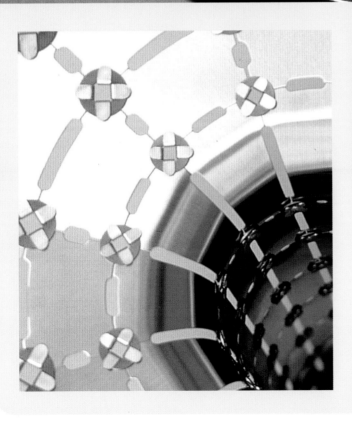

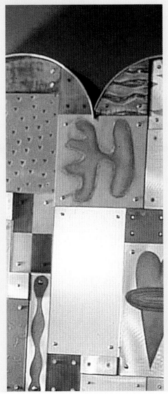

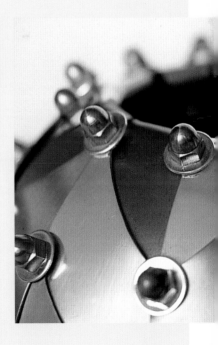

Frankie Flood *PFL (Pizza for Life)*, 2002. 4 x 9½ x 1½ inches (10.2 x 24.1 x 3.8 cm); powder coated aluminum, stainless steel, nickel, ball bearings. Photo by artist

Above: **Harriete Estel Berman** *3M & m Dispenser*, 2001. 6 x 9½ x 2½ inches (15.2 x 24.1 x 6.4 cm); vintage and modern tin cans, recycled tin containers, 10k gold rivets, aluminum rivets, plastic candy dispenser, pre-printed steel. Photo by Philip Cohen

Left: **black+blum** *Mr. & Mrs. Hangup*, 2002. 5¼ x 4⅜ x 1⅝ inches (13 x 11 x 4 cm); brushed stainless steel. Photo by Carolyn Barber

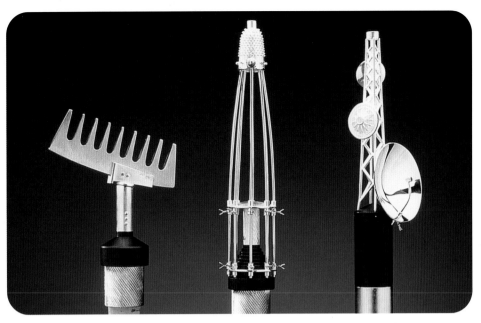

Boris Bally *Combe, Genesis, Dish Bottlecorks,* 2001. 10 x 3¾ x 2 inches (25.4 x 9.5 x 5 cm); silver, ebony, gold plated brass, 18k and 22k gold, cork, ruby; hand-fabricated, cast, lathe-turned, cold-joined, tube-setting. Photo by Dean Powell

Above: **Rebecca Hungerford** *Napkin Rings,* 2003. 1¾ x 1¾ inches (4.5 cm x 4.5 cm) in diameter; pewter; sheet construction, acid-etched design. Photo by artist

Left: **Thomas Mann** *Tech. Tile Elongated Heart Mirror,* 2002. 27 x 63 x ½ inches (68.6 x 160 x 1.3 cm); cold connections; incised, painted, sandblasted, tooled. Photo by Will Crocker

Abrasha *Hanukkah Menorah*, 1997. 6¼ x 14½ x 4¾ inches (15.8 x 36.5 x 12 cm); titanium, stainless steel, socket set screws; machined, fabricated. Photo by Ronnie Tsai

Abrasha *Hanukkah Menorah*, 1995. 7 x 17¼ x 4 inches (17.5 x 43.8 x 9.8 cm); stainless steel, sterling silver, 24k gold; machined, fabricated, soldered, riveted. Permanent collection of the Renwick Gallery of the National Museum of American Art, Smithsonian Institution, Washington, D.C. Photo by Ronnie Tsai

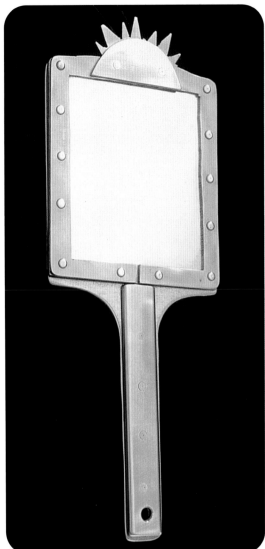

Chuck Russell *Hand Vanity*, 2002. 10 x 4 x 1½ inches (25.4 x 10.2 x .2 cm); aluminum frame, aluminum rivets, stainless steel mirror; rivet assembly. Photo by Christine Rucker

Harriete Estel Berman *In Your Light, I See Light*, 2002–2003. 14½ x 5¼ inches (36.8 x 13.3 cm); recycled tin containers, brass, 10k gold rivets, blue acrylic, pre-printed steel. Photo by Philip Cohen

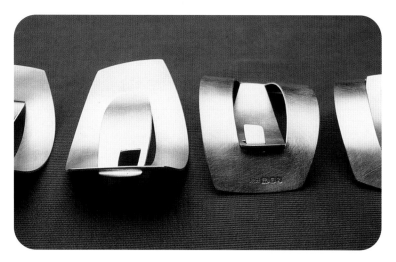

Justine Huntley *Napkin Holders*, 1998. 4 x 2 x 1¼ inches (10 x 5 x 3 cm); silver; pierced, filed, folded, polished, rolled. Photo by P. Harrison

Above: **Joan Morris** *To-Go Box*, 2002. 6½ x 4 x 3½ inches (16.5 x 10.2 x 8.9 cm); aluminum flashing, rivets, wire; cut, folded. Photo by Keith Wright

Right: **Justine Huntley** *Silver Fruit Stand*, 2001. 17¾ x 8 inches (45 x 20 cm); silver; pierced, filed, polished, folded. Photo by P. Harrison

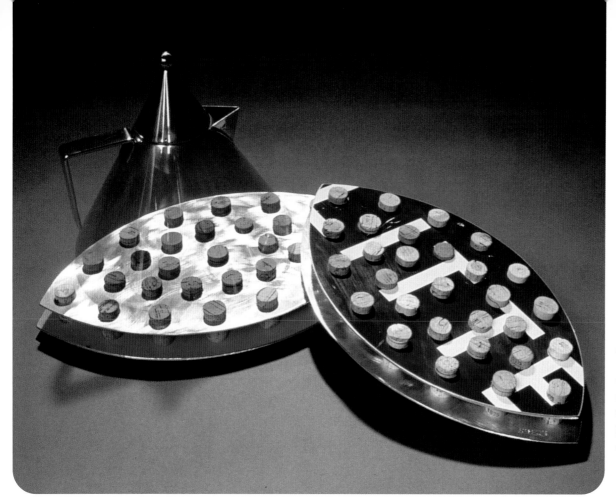

Left: **Boris Bally** *Cork Boat Trivets*, 1999. 15 x 8⅝ x 2 inches (38.1 x 21.9 x 5 cm); re-used bottle corks, traffic signs; fabricated, perforated. Photo by Aaron Usher III

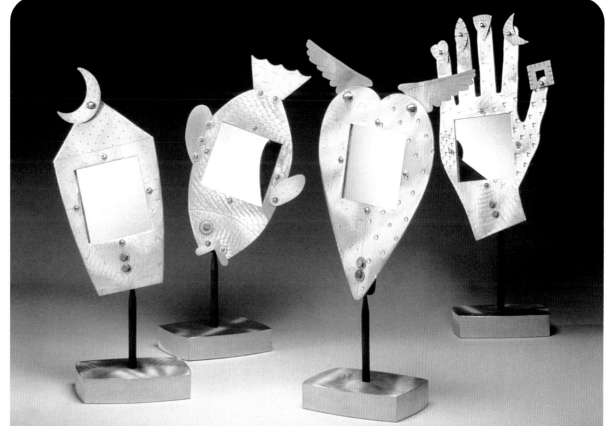

Right:
Thomas Mann
Tech.Reflections, 1999. 20 x 10 x 5 inches (50.8 x 25.4 x 12.7 cm); cold connections; incised, painted, sandblasted, tooled. Photo by Gerard Perrone

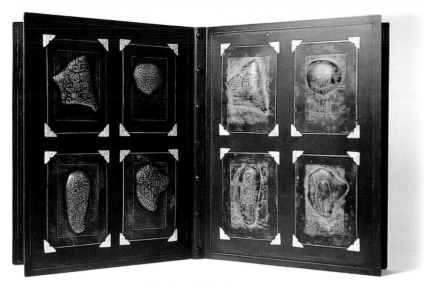

Sandra Noble Goss
Album: At the Beach, 2002. 10 x 8 x 4 inches
(25.4 x 20.3 x 10.2 cm); etched bronze, brass, copper,
sterling silver. Photo by artist

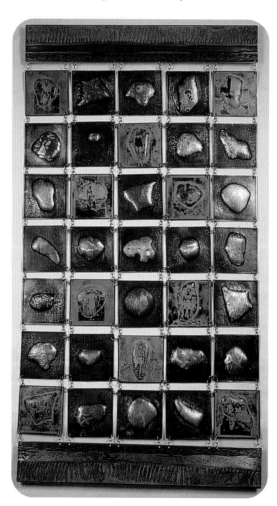

Sandra Noble Goss
Beach Blanket, 2003. 29 x 16 inches (73.7 x 40.6 cm);
etched brass, bronze, sterling silver, patina. Photo by Andrew Goss

Erik Tidäng *Vase*, 2003. 13¾ × 11 × 11 inches (35 × 28 × 28 cm); stainless steel, titanium, glass. Photo by artist

Elizabeth Garvin *Ornaments*, 2003. 2 x 2 x 1¾ inches (5 x 5 x 4.4 cm); acrylic, nickle silver, plastic, leaded crystal, anodized aluminum, sterling silver; riveted construction. Photo by artist

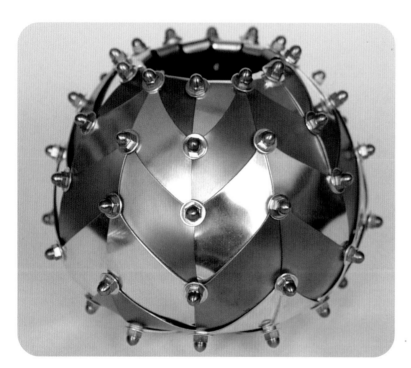

Erik Tidäng *Bowl*, 2001. 6 x 8 x 8 inches (15 x 20 x 20 cm); silver, titanium, brass bolts; scales screwed together. Photo by artist

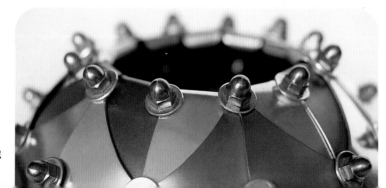

Gallery Artists

Abrasha
San Francisco, California, U.S.A.
www.abrasha.com
Abrasha creates contemporary jewelry from unexpected combinations of precious and non-precious materials in forms well beyond traditional jewelry concepts. His work is exhibited in private collections, galleries, and museums, and is part of the permanent collections of the Smithsonian Institution's Renwick Gallery of the National Museum of American Art and the Oakland Museum.

Boris Bally
Providence, Rhode Island, U.S.A.
www.BorisBally.com
Numerous publications have featured Boris Bally's work and it is permanently exhibited in museums and galleries in Europe and North America, including the Victoria and Albert Museum, the Smithsonian Institution's Renwick Gallery of the National Museum of American Art, Goldschmiedgesellschaft, and the American Crafts Museum. He shares his expertise of metalsmithing and jewelry design with students as an Apprentice Mentor at The Met School in Providence, Rhode Island.

Harriete Estel Berman
San Mateo, California, U.S.A.
www.harriete-estel-berman.info
The materials Harriete Estel Berman uses to construct her work include vintage steel dollhouses and post-consumer, recycled tin containers. For Harriete, careful craftsmanship and thoughtful composition make renewed and endless invention possible as she diverts material from its destiny as trash. Her work is represented by Sybaris Gallery, Mobilia Gallery, Charon Kransen, and Facere Jewelry Art. It is also featured in the permanent collections of the Smithsonian Institution's Renwick Gallery of the National Museum of American Art, Detroit Institute of Arts, The Jewish Museum, and Temple University's Tyler School of Art.

black+blum
London, England
www.black-blum.com
black+blum, an Anglo-Swiss partnership, joined forces in 1998 and based themselves in London. As a design consultancy, they advise companies on many creative aspects. This accumulating insight into different markets catalyzed the decision to also develop their own range of products. black+blum has since become a vehicle to fully explore and enjoy their creativity. Their philosophy shows that "designed" products can be made affordable without compromising quality. They aim to create innovative products that will charm and entertain.

Frankie Flood
Champaign, Illinois, U.S.A.
Frankie Flood's work focuses on functional tools and the reinterpretation of those forms. He began this project after working in an industrial setting, where he observed machinists who were highly capable in their field, but saw no artistic value in their methods or techniques. He has combined industrial and machining processes with contemporary metals design. This has led to an appreciation of everyday objects that can stimulate design, specifically the design of machined functional objects. Frankie Flood is a member of the Society of North American Goldsmiths and exhibits his work in galleries across the United States.

Elizabeth Garvin
New York, New York, U.S.A.
www.elizabethgarvin.com
Elizabeth Garvin combines inspiration from architecture and industrial design with traditional jewelry-making methods to design forms, engineer movement, and develop new techniques for wearable art and home accessories. Her work is exhibited internationally in galleries and museum stores as well as home furnishing and design boutiques.

Sandra Noble Goss

Owen Sound, Ontario, Canada

www.makersgallery.com/goss/

Sandra Noble Goss' recent work examines memory and the passage of time. Her exploration of this theme has resulted in jewelry and etched metal wall pieces which juxtapose images of fossils with old photographs. Working with etched metal in her jewelry led to "beach diaries" in the form of etched and patinated wall pieces. Sandra Noble Goss's metal artwork has been shown in many galleries since 1970. She is represented by Prime Gallery, The Guild Shop of the Ontario Crafts Council, Metalworks, LaFreniere & Pai, Harbinger Gallery, Tom Thomson Gallery, Circle Arts Gallery, Marten Arts Gallery, Burlington Arts Centre, MacLaren Art Centre, Village Studios, 24 Downie Street, Marten Arts Gallery, Inside Gallery, Winnipeg Art Gallery, and the Canadian Craft Museum. She teaches part-time at Georgian College's jewelry program in Barrie, Ontario, and also at Haliburton School of Fine Arts in their summer programs.

Rebecca Hungerford

Kansas City, Missouri, U.S.A.

www.pewtershop.com

Rebecca Hungerford began working with gold, silver, and pewter while still in high school. Following college she moved to the Boston area where she worked for a jeweler, a silversmith, and a stained glass studio. Three years after studying pewtersmithing in Canada, Hungerford returned to her home in northern Ohio. She opened a small shop in Bath, Ohio, in the fall of 1975. During her first 20 years as a pewtersmith, Rebecca primarily focused on designs with traditional themes, but in 1995 she began producing completely new and original works. It was at this time that her art became widely noticed and enthusiastically collected. Her artwork has been displayed in the U.S. and Asia in gallery exhibitions and at craft fairs.

Justine Huntley

London, England

Justine produces functional tableware in a variety of metals, but predominately in silver. For her silver, she imposes an economic use of material. These practical concerns are combined with utilizing the virtues of balance, light, and proportions within the structure. Justine has exhibited at the Nottingham Castle Museum, the Devon Guild of Craftsmen, the Koldinghus Museum, Goldsmiths Hall, Galleria Delle Art, the Leslie Craze Gallery, Thomas Goode and Co., Aspreys', the International Furniture Fair, and the Victoria and Albert Museum.

Thomas Mann

New Orleans, Louisiana, U.S.A

www.thomasmann.com

Thomas Mann is a designer, jeweler, and sculptor who has experimented with collage and assemblage techniques to develop his signature Techno-Romantic® style. His work has received numerous awards and is exhibited in private collections, galleries, and museums, including the American Craft Museum. Thomas has contributed his work for feature in numerous publications, and he is the subject of a new book, *Thomas Mann Metal Artist.*

Joan Morris

Asheville, North Carolina, U.S.A.

Joan Morris' artistic endeavors have led her down many successful creative paths. After studying ceramics, Joan ran her own clay windchime business for 15 years. Since 1993, Joan has owned Vincent's Ear, a downtown coffeehouse in Asheville, North Carolina. As a designer for Lark Books, Joan's projects have been featured in *Beautiful Ribbon Crafts* (Spring 2003), *The Weekend Crafter: Dried Flower Crafts* (Spring 2003), *Gifts for Babies* (Spring 2003), *Halloween: A Grown-up's Guide to Creative Costumes, Devilish Decor & Fabulous Festivities* (Fall 2003), *Hardware Style* (Fall 2003), *Creating Fantastic Vases* (Fall 2003), and *Shelf Expression* (Spring 2004).

Chuck Russell
Plane Art
Winston-Salem, North Carolina, U.S.A
Chuck Russell enjoys working with non-ferrous metals. He uses recycled aircraft metal and parts to fabricate useful items, and most of his connections are made with rivets, bolts, and screws. This cold assembly process is Russell's method of choice, as he uses the same techniques to repair jet aircraft.

Erik Tidäng
Stockholm, Sweden
www.lod.nu
Erik Tidäng finds it fascinating to observe the construction techniques nature uses to create works of immense beauty and strength; often to a degree of accuracy and intricacy that defies modern engineering. He builds his pieces of many small identical or similar elements in order to fashion a larger sculptural body that incorporates a practical as well as an aesthetic function. Born in Göteborg, Tidäng graduated from Konstfack in Stockholm with a masters degree in Metal Design. Erik is a member of Nutida Svenskt Silver. He is a master of mathematics and geometry, a fact that can't be escaped when one becomes absorbed in his work. Erik is represented in Sweden's National Museum.

Templates

Glowing Votive Holder, page 34

Cylinder, template A

Glowing Votive Holder, page 34

Base, template B

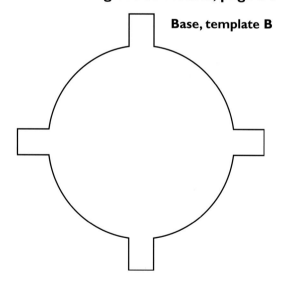

Bubble Switch Plate, page 36

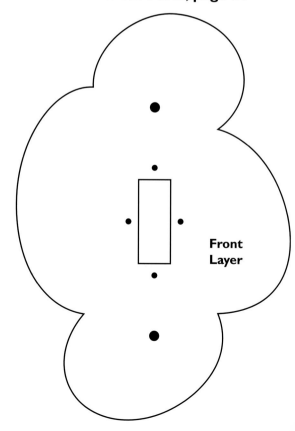

Front Layer

Bubble Switch Plate, page 36

Ginko Leaf Chopstick Rest, page 38

Bubble Switch Plate, page 36

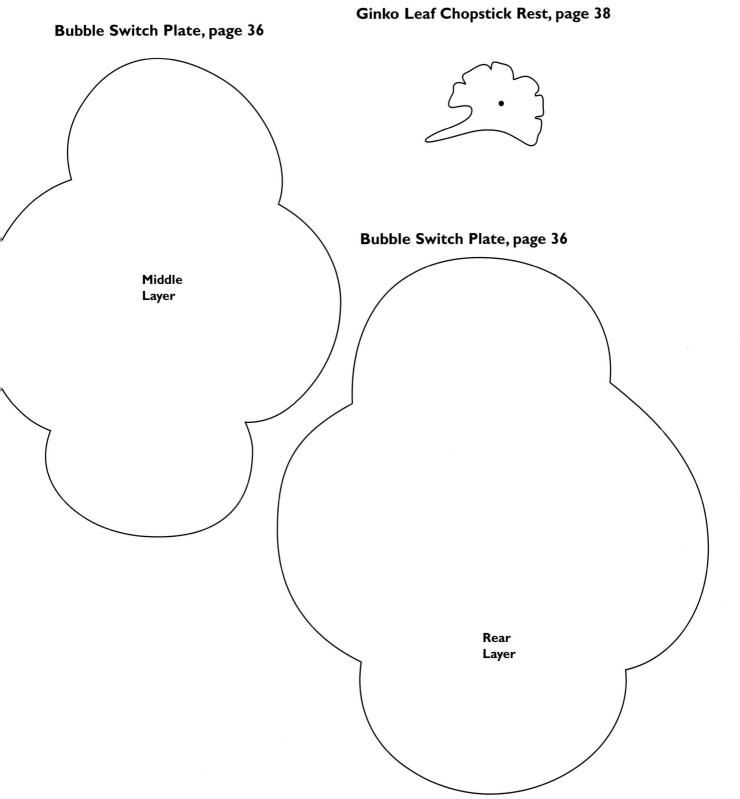

Middle
Layer

Rear
Layer

High-Flying Journal, page 60

Falling Leaf Fan Pull, page 63

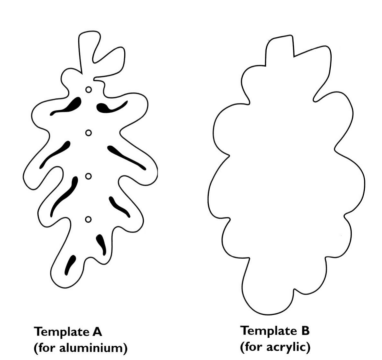

Template A
(for aluminium)

Template B
(for acrylic)

Whimsical Wall Hook, page 70

**Template A
Foot**

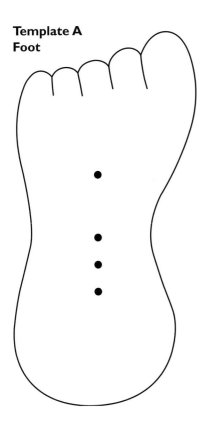

Pushpin Pizzazz, page 47

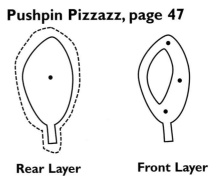

Rear Layer   Front Layer

**Template B
Top Layer (small lotus)**

**Template C
Rear Layer (large lotus)**

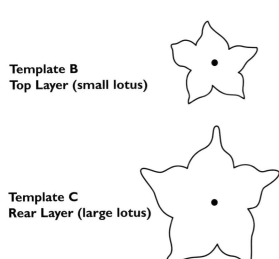

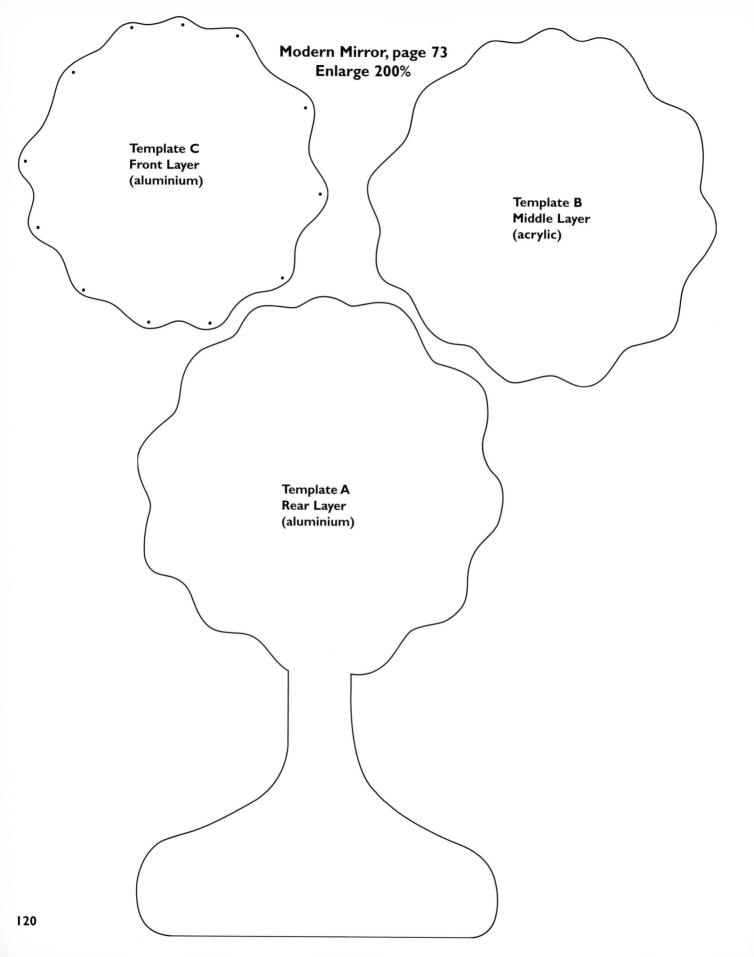

Modern Mirror, page 73
Enlarge 200%

Template C
Front Layer
(aluminium)

Template B
Middle Layer
(acrylic)

Template A
Rear Layer
(aluminium)

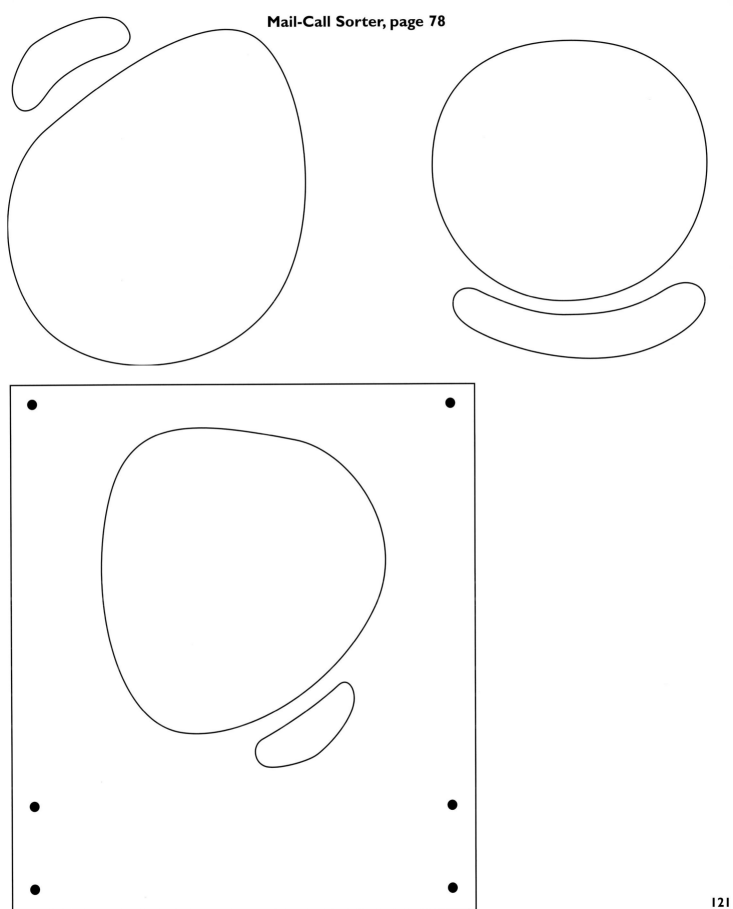

Sparkling Salad Servers, page 81

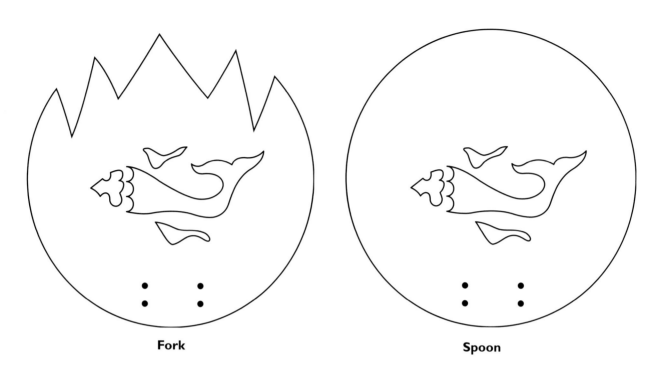

Fork

Spoon

Candle Snuffer, page 87

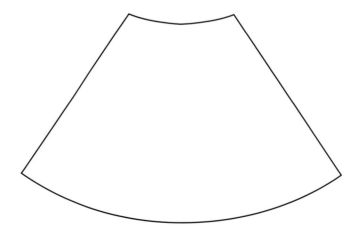

Howl-at-the-Moon Lampshade, page 84

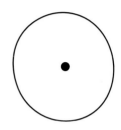

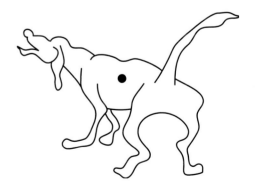

Red Hot Spatula, page 91

Spatula template

Handle template

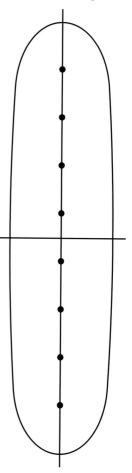

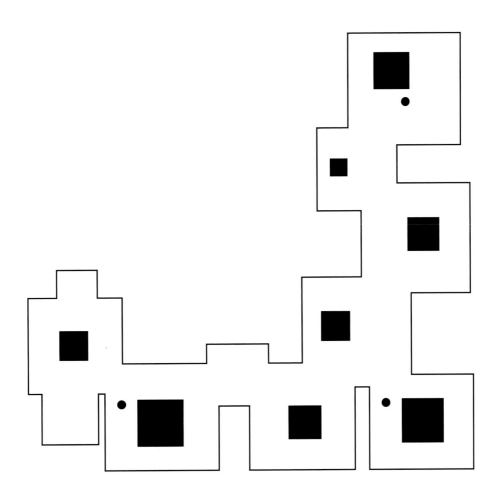

ACKNOWLEDGMENTS

I must give a heartfelt hug of thanks to my editor, Marthe Le Van, for working with me so well, and for helping to make this book clear, easily understood, and a collaborative work of which I can be proud.

Thanks to Geoffrey Giles for giving me much advice and lending me his ears—constantly!

Immense thanks to Sydney Scherr, my very first metalsmithing teacher, who helped show me that making things from metal can bring mental peace. I never knew before her class that time could pass in such a lovely way.

Thanks to Pamela Lins for introducing plastics and alternative materials into my materials repertoire. That kind of use of color really makes me happy.

A big thank you to the gallery artists for sharing their work and giving inspiratiion.

Thanks to Keith and Wendy Wright, the most excellent photography team.

And of course, much thanks to all the folks at Lark Books, especially Susan McBride for her creative art direction.

INDEX

GALLERY ARTIST INDEX

Notes about Suppliers

Usually, the supplies you need for making the projects in Lark books can be found at your local craft supply store, discount mart, home improvement center, or retail shop relevant to the topic of the book. Occasionally, however, you may need to buy materials or tools from specialty suppliers. In order to provide you with the most up-to-date information, we have created a listing of suppliers on our website, which we update on a regular basis. Visit us at www.larkbooks.com; click on "Craft Supply Sources"; and then click on the relevant topic. You will find numerous companies listed with their website address and/or mailing address and phone number.